the Crafty Superstar Ultimate Craft Business Guide

By
GRACE DOBUSH

NORTH
LIGHT
BOOKS

CINCINNATI, OHIO

CONTENTS

Introduction

STATE OF THE CRAFTY UNION

Since the first edition of *Crafty Superstar* came out in 2009, a lot of stuff has changed.

More people than ever before are selling their crafts online, which makes it more challenging to get noticed. More makers are applying to sell at craft shows, which makes it more difficult to get accepted. On top of all that, the economy's remained in the dumps, and everything's gotten more expensive.

But it's not all bad news. Crafters have more options than ever before for online marketplaces, payment processing services and craft shows. Customers have become more familiar with the handmade ethos, and many more people are specifically seeking out eco-friendly and ethically-made products. People want to support their local artisans and businesses.

Some of the crafters featured in the first *Crafty Superstar* book have gone through changes since then. Some have stepped back from the craft world, and a few have become even bigger superstars.

I've been through work and life changes myself. I'm now the community manager for two major design magazines, and I've been traveling to speak at creative business conferences around the country. With a friend, I started an indie craft show here in Cincinnati, and we put on two huge shows every year—in addition to our day jobs. I've sold my handbound books and linocut cards at some of the biggest indie craft shows around the country—some of which have been great and some of which have not. But I've discovered that, for me, interacting with people face-to-face pays off more (emotionally and financially) than trying to sell my goods online. We've created a real craft community here in the Midwest, one that supports many shows, consignment craft stores and business events—one that I'm proud to be a part of.

So I've updated and revised the material that was included in my first book to make it applicable to craft businesses today. This is a book that can help you get started with your craft business—and grow with you as your business evolves and changes. I've included my favorite small-business resources, the advice of dozens of crafters and helpful tips from experts to help you make your creative business everything you want it to be.

Chapter 1

Do You DIY?

Crafts have gotten so popular in the last decade that sometimes it seems like everybody and their grandma are getting on the business bandwagon. And with the dismal economic environment, lots of folks are seeking secondary (or tertiary) sources of income.

This chapter explores the reasons for the handmade craze and explains some of the terms that get tossed around. You'll also figure out what direction your biz should take by meditating on your motivations and expectations. If you just want to cash in on the handmade trend, you may be disappointed. Profits don't come easy, and there's a lot of competition in the DIY marketplace. If you need to make bucketloads of cash to have fun with craft, your heart isn't in it—and buyers will be able to tell. (And this book isn't for you.) But if you really believe in yourself and the things you create, you should go for it. At worst, you lose a few bucks in Etsy listing fees. At best, you get your crafts into the hands of people around the world and make lots of new crafty friends. Off we go!

WHY HANDMADE?

"The craft world is hotness on top of hotness right now," says Garth Johnson, the man behind the blog Extreme Craft (www.extremecraft.com). Aside from the simple satisfaction that comes from making something yourself, there are a couple major reasons for craft's popularity.

People appreciate the personal relationships they have with makers. Lauren Bacon, co-author of *The Boss of You*, says the small scale of the craft business is what's important about crafting. "Artisanry is so incredibly valuable now because it keeps us in touch with real human relationships," she says. "When I wear the earrings I bought, I've got a relationship with the person who made them."

Johnson agrees that the rise of crafts stems from a need for community. "I give most of the credit for craft momentum to the organizers behind major craft fairs like Renegade, Art vs. Craft and Felt Club. These are alpha organizers who connected loose groups of people together."

Buying handmade is also a stylish alternative to sweatshops and mass-produced goods. The tagline for Cinnamon Cooper's business, Poise.cc, is, "I'd rather carry a heavy purse than a heavy conscience." She goes to great lengths to make sure all her materials are sweatshop-free. "The interfacing I use is from a company in Germany, and I want all my cottons grown, dyed and printed in the US," Cooper says.

Nobody knows about the rise of the indie craft scene better than Faythe Levine, whose documentary, *Handmade Nation*, and its accompanying book captured a major moment in handmade history. "The exciting thing about craft and DIY is that everyone can do it," she says. "There's no one saying that you have to do it one way; it's about having the creative urge and following through with it. Deciding what you want to do with it afterward is up to you."

WHAT'S "INDIE"?

Indie, DIY, handmade—there are a lot of different descriptors for the hip things craftsters are creating and selling. You can discuss the semantics for ages, and some people do. (I dare you to ask "What is indie?" at a craft business gathering.) Some people say screen-printed T-shirts aren't handmade enough to be DIY. Others include vintage wares under the indie umbrella. Some exclude items created with mainstream craft supplies. Some indie crafts are one-of-a-kind. Some are made entirely from scratch. Some blur the line between fine art and traditional craft. Some blur the line between trash and treasure.

I think of "indie" (stemming from independent) as the visual contradiction of combining granny craft techniques with punk sensibilities. A classic example of indie craft (that's been completely co-opted by big-box stores, by the way) is a knit scarf with pink skulls on it.

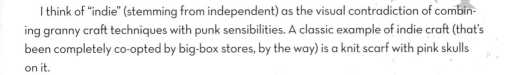

> Part of the joy is the awkwardness and obtuseness of the word *craft*. To some people, it means pom-poms and pipe cleaners, and to others, a perfectly made wooden rocking chair by Sam Maloof.

—Garth Johnson

Indie craft is really similar to indie music in terms of exclusivity—and irony. When it's underground and exclusive, the look has the organic street cred corporate types salivate over. Eventually, the trend catches on with the general public, gets diluted and overdone, and by that point, it's totally over. "One of the last craft fairs that I visited, the Indie Craft Experience in Atlanta, had a bunch of representatives from big companies that flew down to sniff out the newest trends," Johnson says. "I always have an intense love-hate reaction when I walk down the Martha Stewart aisle at Michael's. All of the craft supplies are achingly hip and perfect, but they're being culled and developed by a mega-corporation."

Johnson chooses not to define craft. "Part of the joy is the awkwardness and obtuseness of the word. To some people, it means pom-poms and pipe cleaners, and to others, a perfectly made wooden rocking chair by Sam Maloof. At every craft conference, people beat their chests and complain about how craft needs to be defined for everybody to move ahead. I think just the opposite," Johnson says. "Indie craft is just as prickly. For some, it's synonymous with 'sloppy craft' and lack of attention to detail. While indie crafters are certainly more cavalier about craftsmanship, I think craftsmanship is becoming more important as crafters get older and gain more experience."

When it comes down to figuring out whether you fit into a scene or under the indie umbrella, the most important thing is to stay true to your ideals and aesthetic. Who says you need a label, anyway?

Indie Craft Trends

In 2009, Garth Johnson said: "After some careful analysis, I think brass knuckles are the new octopi, which were the new owls, which were the new sparrows. Check it out! There are about 200 different brass-knuckle–related items on Etsy right now. Sell your stock in octopi and jump on the brass knuckles train."

Indie craft trends never cease to amuse me: One maker will use a kooky (often vintage-inspired) motif on a bag or T-shirt, and next thing you know, it's at every craft show and then finally pops up at Target and H&M. My web developer friend Paul Henrich and I created the site Crafts are the New Crafts (www.craftsarethenewcrafts.com) to poke fun at the craft trends popping up.

And then I made my Indie Craft Trend Engine, an analog version of the website. I built this "engine" out of a shoebox, poster tubes and an oatmeal canister. People can turn the knobs to come up with a prediction about what the next big craft trend will be. (Ibexes are the new sparrows? Arugula are the new cupcakes? Mustaches are the new mustaches?) And then, for $3, I print their pairing on a card with hand-carved stamps.

MOTIVATIONS

Before you decide to cross over from casual crafter to crafty superstar, you should consider two things: your motivations for selling your stuff and your expectations of what will happen when you take your wares to market.

I think the most awesome thing about crafting is the fact that you're your own boss and get to decide what's important to you. Buying and selling handmade gets us further off the grid with each ironic tea cozy and every pair of made-to-order mittens. We know the creation of the product has violated no human rights laws and that its maker was fairly compensated. We can rise above consumer culture and free ourselves from the shackles of big-box stores!

In 2003, Cinnamon Cooper had been making bags for about two years and giving them away to nonprofits for auctions and raffles. She got such glowing feedback and so many requests to buy them that she decided to try to start a business where she'd sell bags and put the profits toward charities she wanted to support but hadn't been able to afford to on her own.

Olivera Bratich's start in the craft business also came through making crafts to raise funds for projects and organizations. "At some point, I looked around and saw a lot of friends who were making really interesting things but had no place in town to sell them," she says. She ended up starting the shop Wholly Craft in Columbus, Ohio. "I started the business with the mission to help people sustain themselves through creative endeavors. These days, I still do some crafting myself—a mix of knitting, papercraft and jewelry making—but most of the time, I'm focused on keeping the shop stocked full of other people's awesome work." And Bratich still holds another job—by day she works in public health, coordinating community planning around HIV/AIDS care.

Hannah Howard started her shop, Lizzie Sweet, because she saw an unfilled need in the beauty market. "I started making perfume because I'm asthmatic. I love things that smell good, but not everything that smells good loves me," she says. "I got into mixing perfume oils, and other people asked for some, too. Lizzie Sweet was born from making and selling things for friends. I like sharing what I do with other people. Making money is not the cake; it's the cherry."

Susie Ghahremani of boygirlparty started her illustrated paper goods business because she liked making things and it was fun to come up with products and new drawings. She says, "Eventually making a living, creating a brand and helping the environment became motivators for me, but not initially. I was just a hyperactive college student when I started."

Jesse Breytenbach on . . .
Motivations

Jesse Breytenbach is an illustrator and crafter in South Africa who makes beautiful hand-printed fabrics and many other things under the name Henri Kuikens.

"I think if I only wanted to make money, there are far less complicated ways of doing so. When I discovered craft forums on the Internet, I just wanted to be part of that sharing of ideas. Profit does come into it—I price my goods to make money, partly to keep in line with other crafters and partly because I think it's only worth doing if it is actually profitable. I'd love to make a living doing only what I love, but I'm not ready to give up my day job completely.

"I'm also not sure that I'm the kind of person who can work out what will sell and refine that to come up with a line of products judged purely for profit. Part of my love of crafting is just that—a love. I enjoy making new things, and I particularly enjoy figuring out how to make them. I often take inspiration from my own life, making what I need or want, which is probably not the best business model.

"Helping the environment is a background motivation—I make things on a small scale and pretty much stick to what I can make myself, producing as little waste as possible. I try to use found or vintage fabrics—my initial motivation for block-printing fabric was a 'no waste' one. I didn't want to have silkscreened yardage that I might not use; I thought if I could create a few motifs that I could print in different patterns as I needed them, even cutting out the pieces of fabric for a bag first, and then printing, I'd be able to save fabric."

What Drives Your Craft?

Try this checklist on for size—check as many motivations as apply.

☐ Making a profit

☐ Making a living

☐ Having fun

☐ Creating a brand

☐ Serving a cause

☐ Helping the environment

☐ Growing your local economy

☐ Other: _____

These are all good reasons to try to take your crafting to the next level. One of them or some of them may apply to you. Or you can make up your own motivation. Whatev! Just be sure your business plan matches up with your motivations.

EXPECTATIONS

After you've chewed on your motivations for a while, it's time to take stock and think about what you'd like your business to look like and if you can really make it happen.

Would I have fun crafting for others instead of myself?

That beaded cochlear coin purse you fussed over for so many hours will go home with someone else after the craft show. Can you bear to never see it again? It's a little like giving away kittens. Rough, dude. If you're accustomed to giving away all your creations for birthdays and holidays, you'll probably be fine. If you've stashed away every amigurumi you ever hooked, you might have a problem.

Would I have fun making similar things over and over?

Unless you specialize in one-offs, you'll likely find a few things that sell like gangbusters, and you'll craft to meet the demand. This can mean long nights and a lackluster social life, plus putting your personal projects on the back burner. It could also mean developing a repetitive stress injury. That's why finding joy in crafting is so important. You don't want to lock yourself up like you're in the Triangle Shirtwaist Factory until you perish in the flames of your crafty desire.

Do I have the cash to beef up my output?

Buying more fabric, paper and rickrack might not be so bad, but what if you need a heavy-duty sewing machine, a ginormous printer or an industrial-revolution-size loom? These are things to consider before you bite off more than you can sew. If you're serious about growing your biz, a loan might be something to consider. Or it might mean dipping into savings, reworking your household budget or canceling cable. If you have no pennies to pinch, it's time to get creative in your approach to production. Look into renting equipment or studio time, or reconsider the way you make things. Do you really need virgin wool, or can you use thrift store sweaters? Upcycling is a great way to cut costs, and it's a great selling point for your goods.

What makes my product stand out from the crowd?

It doesn't matter whether your main medium is normal knitting or a welding-origami hybrid—another crafter is probably rockin' it, too. But the difference between craft biz and traditional business is that the conflicting interest doesn't necessarily make you mortal enemies. What you're really selling is your personal aesthetic. So your personal style should shine through in everything you make—that's what draws people to handmade stuff. Little details are what can make a product go from being just another mustache-on-a-stick to the must-have novelty of the summer.

Is there an audience for my work?

How many people are in the market for a life-size felted bust of Andrew McCarthy? I mean, really. The great thing about the Internet is that even the wackiest stuff will find a buyer, but there's a certain level of appeal required to be able to sell your stuff with any frequency. If you're OK with serving the small but dedicated group of Brat Pack devotees or just don't feel like going mainstream, that's totally cool.

What do I expect to happen when I put my crafts out in the world?

There are always going to be haters. Can you take the heat? At my first craft show, I made less than $20. Though subsequent shows have been much more successful, I can still count on overhearing someone sniff, "$30 for that?" It can also be overwhelming to encounter crafters whose work is similar to yours—especially if you're selling at the same show. Have confidence in your work and yourself, and you'll be fine.

What makes a crafter successful depends on your definition of success and how you want to achieve it. The three following characteristics will be useful no matter your M.O.: self-confidence, self-motivation and killer organizational skills.

"If you want to be successful, first you must believe in yourself with all your might," plush purveyor Jenny Harada says. "Being doubtful will get you nowhere. Put everything into it that you can. It will be hard work, but it will be yours, all yours, and worth it."

Running a crafty biz means being a Jill of all trades, and you have to be a real self-starter (if you'll pardon the business jargon). The wonderful part of being your own boss is that the biz becomes your baby—you want it to flourish and strive, and I think you'll find that nurturing it comes naturally.

After you've meditated on your motivations and expectations for a little while, you're ready to take your first steps toward becoming a crafty superstar:

1. Pick a name.

2. Google your name to make sure nobody is using it. If somebody else has it, repeat Step 1.

3. Profit!

OK, so maybe it's not that simple to become a crafty superstar. But it's a place to start. Take some time to fill out the next few pages with your vision for your business.

> If you want to be successful, first you must believe in yourself with all your might.
>
> —Jenny Harada

What's your elevator pitch?
Describe what you make in one paragraph.

How would you describe your brand?

What other creative businesses do you admire?

How would you like your brand to be regarded?

What's the definition of success for you?

If you could accomplish just one thing with
your business, what would it be?

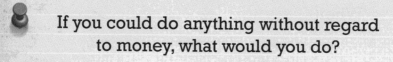

If you could do anything without regard
to money, what would you do?

When you were eighteen, where did
you think you would be now?

How about when you were eight?

Chapter 2

Biz Basics

Since most of us start making crafts as a hobby, sometimes it's hard to think about our passion for macramé, lamination or weldigami as a business. (And I'm not even going to start in on the whole left-brain/right-brain thing.) But if you want to be taken seriously—and you do if you wanna get paid—you gotta put down the knitting needles and do some homework.

In this section, we'll go over the deets on naming your crafty business and figuring out what you should charge for your goods. I've got some strategies for boosting production and setting up an optimal workspace, too. And we'll finally get down to the nitpicky details on how to keep your business legal. I'm not a lawyer or a tax adviser, but I'll send you in the right direction to start your business on the up and up.

SETTING UP

If you want people to take you seriously, you've got to consider your business seriously. These simple first steps will get your crafty biz ready to go live.

The name game

When it comes to picking a name, you have to make sure the one you want is actually available. Search on Google and Etsy for businesses and crafters with similar names. For example, you don't want to pick a name like Sublime Stitchery when there's already a Sublime Stitching. It's also worth it to check the database of the US Patent and Trademark Office (www.uspto.gov) to make sure nobody's using the name you want at the national level. And try it out as a dot-com to see if anyone else already has the domain.

It's wise to avoid an overly descriptive name that might hinder you from expanding your business. For example, you wouldn't expect Barbaric Berets to sell anything other than violently French hats. Holly Klump, who ran a business called misshawklet, advises, "Never name your business after your username! All your old posts from message boards will come up when people google you."

If you're setting up as a sole proprietorship (which anybody doing business alone automatically is) but are using a descriptive name for your biz, you have to register your fictitious name. This is called Doing Business As (DBA) or Operating As (OA), and it's done at the local, county or state level, depending on where you live.

> **Never name your business after your username! All your old posts from message boards will come up when people google you.**
>
> —Holly Klump

When you pick your name and have ensured that no one else has it, register the Internet domain name, even if you're only planning on selling on Etsy for now. You can set up the URL to redirect to your Etsy store. Through a registrar such as Name.com, you can get your own dot-com domain for as little as $10.

You've got (to get) mail

Set up a business e-mail address (I'm all about Gmail—the inbox size limits are insane) to keep your biz stuff separated from your personal or work e-mail. Also, since your e-mail address should be easy to find on your website, it may result in more spam, and you don't want to junk up your personal e-mail inbox if you don't have to. Go ahead and set up a PayPal account at www.paypal.com with that e-mail address while you're at it.

Consider getting a post office box if you'll be doing a lot of mail orders and you'd prefer not to put your home as the return address on all your packages. A post office box can cost as little as $10 for a six-month term.

Scope out your business

And now to wrap up some of the last piddling details. You have to nail down the scope of your business. Unless you think a loan application is in your future, you probably don't have to develop a full-blown business plan at this point. Use the questionnaire on the next page to flesh out your business idea and give it life.

FYI

You can find an accredited list of dot-com registrars at www.icann.org/en/registrars/accredited-list.html.

Setting Up Shop Questionnaire

What are you going to make and sell?

....
....
....
....

Where do you want to sell it?

....
....
....
....

Who's your competition, and what are they up to?

....
....
....
....

How much money do you need to get started?

....
....
....
....

How much time do you expect to devote to the business?

....
....
....
....

PRICING

Pricing is a terrifically tricky area. When you're first starting out it's tempting to charge just what you spent on materials, but don't sell yourself short. Charging for the time you spent making each item might make your sticker price seem high, but a person who makes things by hand can't compete with big-box stores' prices. Most people are so far removed from the manufacturing process that they have no idea of what making something really costs.

Customer perceptions

One thing's for sure: If you price your work too low, customers will wonder if it is cheap, and that's no good. In crafting, pricing your work low isn't going to increase demand. Honestly, at an indie craft show you'll see more people buying $5 letterpress cards than flimsy cards that cost 50 cents. Generally, the misers who complain about high prices at shows don't appreciate the hard work it takes to make something by hand. Pay them no mind—they weren't gonna buy from you anyway.

Lauren Bacon, the co-author of *The Boss of You*, a business guide aimed at women, likes to say that handmade goods' high prices aren't high—they're just the real price. "The organic local food industry is a good example of this. Local artisan cheese is so much more expensive than imported cheese," she says. "The cool thing about indie economies is that you get to talk to the people who made it and ask them yourself why it costs what it does. All of those things have real, concrete value."

When you're selling at craft fairs or through Etsy, you can start a dialogue with your customers about pricing and why you charge what you do. "Instead of being afraid, look at the crafters who are established and are charging what they're worth. Ask them how they set their prices, if for no other reason than moral support," Bacon says. "If you're going to a big craft show where a lot of people's prices are lower than yours, practice your answers about why your prices are so high. Have fun with it—make a little FAQ and put it on your table, even. Explain that you use sustainable materials, or that your stitching is time-intensive and impeccable and long-lasting. Engaging with your customers is what gives your product value, because they care about the item, but they also care about their relationship with you."

There are always going to be people whose bottom line is price. They're not your target market, and that's a hard thing for people who love their work to let go. "You'll make compromises and excuses to keep doing what you love," Bacon says. "But look at yourself as an employee and ask, 'Is it reasonable to be paying myself $7 an hour for this?'"

Setting your prices

Crafters who sell their products go about setting their prices in different ways. For instance, Jessica Manack of Miss Chief Productions has a simple method to price her items. "When I'm creating a product, the first thing I do after I make a prototype is look all over the Internet to see where I can get the materials to make it," she says. "The materials I find partly determine whether I go ahead with making it. I went ahead with the magnet tins I make because of the tins I found." She calculated their price based on how many she could make in an hour. But she's recently reconsidered this—read about her pricing experiment on page 32.

Samantha Lopez of Knotstudio based her prices on the cost of precious metals and the time-intensive process required to make her jewelry. "I knew coming into this that in the long run it'd be much harder to raise prices than to lower them if they were too high," she says. "I first did a lot of research on the stores that would potentially carry my line and the prices of work they carried. Based on that, I saw that my niche in this case was going to be the rather high-end luxury goods market." Lopez adjusts her prices occasionally, mostly to follow the metal market. "It's important to keep in mind that, although lowering the prices may attract new customers, established clients may feel they were ripped off and take their business elsewhere. Lately, because of the economy, I've decided to keep my smaller silver pieces and offer the larger, more expensive ones only in gold—not only as a luxury but also an investment, as gold tends to hold its value." Her retail prices are simply double the wholesale prices, which is a standard practice.

Speaking of wholesale, if you even have a single thought of selling wholesale, Bacon advises considering that when setting your retail prices. "Let's say the break-even price you find for your product is $50. When you're a product-based business, you have to think about wholesale price as well as retail. Because there will be a time when some store comes and asks you what your wholesale prices are, and they're going to expect a big discount from your retail price—usually 50 percent. So if you're selling an item for $60 and somebody wants to buy it wholesale for $30, you're losing money."

However you decide to set your prices, it's important to consider all your costs when figuring out your prices as well as how you will sell items (e.g., in sets or individually)—an hourly rate to pay yourself, the cost of materials, administrative stuff, taxes. And don't forget extra things like listing fees, transaction fees and shipping materials and charges.

Let's get down to the nitty-gritty of all those extra costs for a minute. Pretend you're selling a card on Etsy for $2. It's made from upcycled materials (read: free) and took you fifteen minutes to make. You charge 50 cents for shipping, and you accept payments via PayPal. When it sells, you just made a profit of $2.50, right?

Wrong. Etsy charges 20 cents per listing, plus 3.5 percent of the sale price—so that's 27 cents gone. Then, PayPal charges 30 cents per transaction, plus 2.9 percent of the money received—that's another 37 cents. Assuming you already have an envelope, you still gotta buy a stamp, another 45 cents. So your buyer sent you $2.50, but in reality, you've only made $1.41 from the sale. And since it took you 15 minutes to make the card (and not including the time you spent to list the item and go to the post office), your average hourly wage is $5.64. Those little charges add up, and that's why I sell my linocut cards on Etsy only in packs and generally don't list anything for less than $10—otherwise, the fees would eat up all my profit.

FYI

You can easily estimate your postage costs nationally and internationally with the US Postal Service calculator at postcalc.usps.com. If you're shipping from Canada, you can find rates at www.canadapost.ca/Personal/RatesPrices.

How do you know if your price is right?

Jessica Manack of Miss Chief Productions did an experiment recently to see if her prices were too low. She was inspired to investigate when she saw a business selling 1-inch magnets for $5 each.

She usually sells her magnets for a dollar each, so "I thought I would try listing some on eBay," she says. "I first tried this on Thanksgiving weekend and sold 33 sets for $430." Considering she usually sells sets of nine magnets for $7, that's not shabby! "Everything I have listed has sold, and some people have gone to my Etsy shop after buying stuff on eBay and bought more things. Most of the buyers are from the US, but I have also had some from Australia, South Korea and other places."

Manack thinks part of the increased selling price is because of the bidding war aspect—"People hate losing a contest!"—but it's also likely that her goods were underpriced to begin with. "What is something worth?" she asks. "Whatever someone is willing to pay for it."

PRICING STRATEGIES FOR CREATIVE TYPES

When you're running a creative business, even if it's not your sole source of income, the basis of all pricing is your hourly rate. When you're running a small business, you touch every item you sell or service you offer. Your hard work is what creates the value in your products, so it's super important to never discount yourself.

Thinking about how your creative business fits in your annual income, you might decide, based on your needs and your town's cost of living, you're cool with $15 an hour. But if you're living in an expensive place or trying to cover all the costs an employer would usually cover (like health insurance, taxes and a retirement account), your hourly rate might be much higher. (If you offer a professional service, research the going rates of other professionals in your area. For certain types of creative businesses, flat fees for projects make more sense financially.)

When you've determined the hourly rate you want, that's the basis for everything you sell. For a physical product, your price must include your cost of labor (your hourly rate times how many hours it takes), your material cost, overhead and markup.

Overhead is making sure all of your business costs are covered. Let's say, over the course of a year, you have $5,000 in overhead, including business licenses, accountant fees, craft show application fees, website hosting, equipment costs, software licenses and the like. Divide it out over the year (assuming you base it on a 40-hour workweek), and it comes out to $2.40 an hour.

Markup is your profit. If you want your business to grow, markup is what supports you and protects you. Markups aren't fun, but retail theft, loss and breakage are very real risks for a creative business. Or if your business is service-based, there's the chance a deadbeat customer will stiff you. Applying markup to all of your products ensures bad luck won't put you out of business. Markup is usually 1.5 or 2 times your product's material, labor and overhead costs. And that puts you at your wholesale price. Double that again to get your retail price. (See detailed price calculators on page 182.)

More than likely, the price you come up with for your goods will be more than their made-in-China counterparts. And this is when you have to start having honest conversations with people about why your goods are priced like they are. Keep the conversation positive, and don't apologize for your prices. Sometimes customers can be rude, but resist any urge you have to get hostile.

This is the time for you to highlight what makes your goods valuable and different from mass-produced versions. When they buy from you, they're supporting a locally owned business, a small business, a real person standing in front of them. If you source your supplies locally, ethically or in an environmentally sound manner, that's also worth mentioning.

Always remember: You are worth it!

Cinnamon Cooper on . . . Pricing

My time is worth money. I've worked for years to learn how to improve the quality of my bags. I spend time seeking out sweatshop-free materials, and I make sure that the materials I use will withstand wear and tear. I try to make bags that are attractive as well as functional, and that effort deserves to be compensated. However, when I price out my bags and come up with a final price of what a bag is worth, I think about whether I would save my money for a month to purchase the bag. If I wouldn't, I don't make it again. I want people to feel like they're getting something valuable, but my bags are far from the luxury pricing models.

THREE REASONS WHY DISCOUNTS ARE DEADLY

"$22 for $35 worth of letterpress cards!" "Handmade jewelry for 45% off!" "BOGO screenprinted onesies!" I get so mad when I encounter crafters selling their wares at ridiculous discounts. And recently a spate of handmade discounting schemes has popped up, making me fear the Walmartization of handmade has begun.

Some sites like Groupon for handmade goods have popped up in the last few years. Vendors apply to offer a deal—which often must be at least 50 percent off. One site offered "one unique handpicked item per day at a great value." It's the "great value" part that smacks of big-box discounters to me. Is craftsmanship not worth paying full price for? And Etsy introduced coupon functionality on the site in 2010—now it's all too easy to offer free shipping or a 20 percent discount.

Modern shoppers are primed to react to discounts. (If you're into social history, I highly recommend Ellen Ruppel Shell's book *Cheap: The High Cost of Discount Culture*.) But discounts are largely a phenomenon of the era of mass production—it pains me to see handmade items' prices slashed like outlet mall jeans. Will discounts boost your Etsy sales? Maybe. But I think they'll do crafters much more harm than good in the long run, for these three reasons.

1. Discounts make you undervalue your time.

Crafters are already notorious at underselling themselves. Too often, we simply price our goods at what we consider the going rate, rather than taking into consideration the cost of materials plus the cost of our time and any overhead we have. I fully believe in making a living wage, and I believe every crafter should do the same. More than likely, you're already selling your work for too little. If you discount it any further, you could even be losing money.

When dozens of people are selling similar things on Etsy, you may think you have to lower your prices to compete. But I think people are actually more likely to save up $55 to buy a pair of steampunk owl earrings that they really love than spend $5 on a pair that's marked down from $10.

2. Discounts don't draw the kind of customers you want to have an LTR with.

You might think a buck's a buck, but fair-weather shoppers who only buy when an item is cheap aren't the kind of customers you can count on. Discounts don't create repeat customers—they only create buyers who expect more sales.

If you consistently offer discounts on your handmade items, what incentive does a shopper have to ever pay full price? We need to focus on educating buyers of handmade items as to why our products are priced how they are and why they're worth it. Creating personal connections with customers is what handmade is all about.

If you're struggling to make sales, maybe you don't have a solid idea of who your audience is yet. Do your products appeal more to college students or empty-nest moms? Spendthrift yuppies or up-and-coming country folks? When you know who your customers are, you can figure out how to best reach them, and what prices they'll pay. Discounts won't do that for you. (Learn more about customer profiling on page 162.)

3. Discounts cheapen your work.

Let's face it: Most handmade goods are luxuries. They're lovely nonessentials that people buy because they want to—no matter whether it's because they want to support a small business, to consume more ethically or simply to have beautiful things. When you're a craftsperson, being the cheapest isn't going to help your business. Making quality products—and pricing accordingly—will.

Think about it this way—do you want to be a discount store shampoo brand, selling economy-size bottles of shampoo for $2 with a 25-cent-off coupon? Creative business people are better off following the lead of Aveda, making and selling high-quality, beautiful products that attract a clientele that doesn't need a discount incentive to be convinced to buy from you.

If your customers are sensitive to price, make sure that your pricing strategy can handle the discounts you want to offer. (But you surely see that raising your prices in order to offer discounts is just silly.) One thing I really don't advise is offering free shipping—this is just taking money out of your own pocket. You can't avoid the cost of shipping or do anything to change it. (And free shipping is one big reason why many new companies fail.)

If you feel the need to offer some kind of incentive to your customers—and certainly some customers are more price averse than others—consider offering a freebie with a purchase. This could be a pinback button, a notecard, a mini-size sample or something else that's attractive to your audience.

BOOSTING PRODUCTION

If you're going big time, those six-packs of googly eyes and your weekly craft-while-watching-*House* schedule probably aren't going to cut the mustard anymore.

Buying all your materials in small quantities from retail craft stores isn't usually a sustainable business plan; doing so will eat up your profits. Search the Internet for your most-used materials—scour Google, eBay, Etsy and other online retailers. You almost always find better deals when you buy in bulk. This means snapping up enough glass jars, googly eyes and grommets to last you six months instead of just buying what you need whenever you get an order. Buying in bulk will help you keep your expenses and prices down.

And there's no shame in being a scavenger. Hit up every garage sale and Goodwill in the tri-state area for materials. Jenny Harada, who makes kooky stuffed animals, says, "I buy lots of clothes at thrift shops for the sake of repurposing the fabrics. You can get lots of unique material that way!" Keeping an eye on Craigslist (www.craigslist.org) and Freecycle (www.freecycle.org) is also great for finding used goods. Just keep in mind the usual warnings about making Internet transactions—meet in a public place, pay in cash when you have the goods in hand, and back out if things seem fishy.

Hannah Howard tries to keep the packaging consistent for her line of Lizzie Sweet body products, but her suppliers sometimes discontinue the jars she uses. "It's hard when you only want to buy a few hundred instead of the huge minimums," she says. So she's had to do a lot of research to find wholesalers who will work with small businesses like hers. "I keep a list of places where I can find things in a bind. It's hard to be consistent with packaging when supply lines are drying up, so I'm focusing on keeping consistent with things that are kind of easy to get."

Julianna Holowka has outsourced some production to keep up with the demand for her Mean Cards. "I was very fortunate to be picked up by two very large retailers recently. For these orders, I shifted production to a local printer," she says. "I chose an independent printer here in Philly with a reputation of being the greenest in the region. Even though those cards are no longer printed by me, I was able to have them printed with soy-based ink and increase the recycled content of my paper—putting out a cleaner product and supporting local business at the same time."

It can be tough to stay motivated to produce goods when you're your own boss. You've still got a "real" job and there are no rules. Everybody's different, but you might have some success in setting small goals for yourself. When I'm working on a big project, I like to draw up a calendar that I hang on the wall to write daily or weekly goals on. Or I create routines to get me into the habit of working on my project on a regular basis. For you, this could be taking your knitting projects to your favorite café to work for a whole afternoon every week or setting aside an hour every morning for your crafts. I think it'd be fun to set up a crafting game where, for example, you have to work on your for-profit crafts every time *Law & Order* comes on TV—you'd be a fiend!

Hannah Howard on . . .
Hiring Help

"Once I started getting large orders, I was completely unprepared for it. For a while I told people that I could only make a limited amount of my products, and they could only order up to a certain amount—until I was able to get a part-time worker.

"One thing I wasn't comfortable with was bringing in people who might take what they learned with me to start their own business. It was hard to find people to work with who were just committed to helping. It was also tough to figure out the legalities for paying them and hiring employees. I never wanted to be 'the man.'

"I've hired friends of friends and paid a daily stipend. I never want to create a sweatshop kind of environment. My personal opinion is that you have to pay people at least $10 an hour, and if you pay less, make up for it in food or goodies. I'm a firm believer that you get what you pay for. You also have to be a good judge of character. I only hire people for a short time, like a few days or a night or two, but I've seen other people not be able to pay enough to keep good employees. And if you're looking for people with flexible hours, the pool is small. Luckily, I knew people with odd schedules, like burlesque artists and freelance makeup artists, who could come help me."

FINDING A GOOD WORKSPACE

It's no fun to have to tear down your kitchen table workshop every time you need to eat. This is a good time to finally clean out the attic or take over the guest bedroom. If you're in a small apartment or are otherwise strapped for space, you can always get crafty with it. Think of your setup like a Murphy bed: Create something that you can stash away as is without a lot of fuss. This could be a low table that fits under your bed or boxes of materials that you can pull out of the closet when it's time to get crafty.

Holly Klump bought a house a few years ago and turned part of the basement into a studio for herself. "I painted it how I wanted to, and there's no computer down here, so I'm not distracted. I think that's important," she says. "In the last apartment, I had a craft room, but this is like my craft dungeon."

Kati Hanimägi has a well-lit room in her house dedicated to Oddball Press. "It's crammed with my cluttered desk, computer, all my inventory, filing cabinets, a work table, flat files and miscellaneous bookcases," she says. "This is where I design, correspond, pack up orders, store products, and tend to the daily accounting tasks. It's not a picture-perfect organized office—it's full of mismatched bookshelves exploding with stuff, abandoned filing cabinets, an old-school teacher's desk covered with paper trays, a sewing table that the fax machine's on, and three different receptacles to hold recycling." The basement holds her small, tabletop letterpress, but the ceiling is low and there's not a lot of room to work.

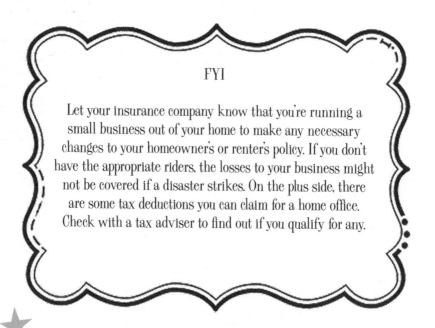

FYI

Let your insurance company know that you're running a small business out of your home to make any necessary changes to your homeowner's or renter's policy. If you don't have the appropriate riders, the losses to your business might not be covered if a disaster strikes. On the plus side, there are some tax deductions you can claim for a home office. Check with a tax adviser to find out if you qualify for any.

If your living space doesn't lend itself to craft production, you might be able to find an artists' co-op or art studio that offers space for a monthly fee or helps with maintenance. (See the sidebar below.) Asking around and googling may turn some up in your area. If there isn't anything that fits your needs, DIY!

Holly Klump on . . .
Creating a Craft Colony

Six months before she moved away, Holly Klump started a group studio in Burlington, Vermont, called Eight Space. To advertise the space, she posted listings on Craigslist and in coffee shops, and in the small town, word spread.

"I was the most productive when I had that space because it was away from my house. I had set hours when I'd go down there and work. Plus, being around other artistic people is a motivation to work on art stuff. It's also nice to have a public space where you can have shows. It's like an artist colony.

"I was like a landlord, subletting to seven other people. It was kinda cool to be in that leadership position. I started a completely separate checking account for it, which was really helpful. To come up with the price, I determined how many people would fit in the space, estimated the utilities and divided by eight and added a little extra. That extra money helped give the group account a little padding for wine for parties so I never was stuck paying for something that wasn't my responsibility.

"Find someone to help you with legal documents for the sublease agreements, and get a security deposit—that came in handy a couple times. You might have to chase people down for the rent—this is where the padding also helped. Leases were for six months, and if someone had to leave early, we kept the deposit if we couldn't find someone to take over their spot. My biggest piece of advice is to be organized and professional about it. When you're dealing with money and people and their stuff, it can get a little weird."

GETTING PAID
AND KEEPING TRACK

And now for the exciting part—getting paid! Even if you're just starting to make sales, you have to approach your income like a pro. Fortunately, this section covers how to accept payments and keep track of things so the IRS doesn't go after your Hobby Lobby receipts.

If you're going to be staying part-time or small-time, a business loan probably isn't in the cards for you just yet. But you do need a business checking account, especially if you plan on accepting checks from customers made out to your business name. Having an account dedicated to your biz also helps in that, with very little effort, you're creating a record of your business's earnings and expenditures. And don't go nuts when you see those digits rising. "The more money you have saved up to launch your business, the better off you will be," Kati Hanimägi says. "Do not buy anything you do not absolutely need. Be smart. Be thrifty!" Note: You'll usually need to show your bank proof of your business structure and tax ID to get a biz checking account. Read more on biz structures on page 43.

Getting paid through PayPal

PayPal is the gold standard for processing payments online. It's integrated with Etsy and eBay, and many other online retailers use it, too. There are three types of accounts—personal, premier and business. A personal account offers only the most basic services; a premier account allows you to accept credit card payments from buyers. With a business account, you can accept payments from customers via your website, via e-mailed invoices or via Virtual Terminal, which works like a credit card swipe machine. Signing up for PayPal is free; the charges come when you receive money from someone. A standard fee is 30 cents per transaction, plus a small percentage. Remember to figure in these costs when setting your prices or shipping charges. (See more about this in the Pricing section on page 29).

If you're using Etsy keep in mind that when you get an order, it's not the same thing as a notification of payment. That comes separately, directly from PayPal. (Make sure your PayPal and Etsy accounts are attached to the same e-mail address—that makes life a lot easier.) If a buyer doesn't send payment within a day or two, send a friendly e-mail letting them know that they still have to pay. Some buyers miss the step unintentionally.

Square

Accepting credit cards used to be a huge ordeal for small business owners. But not anymore, thanks to Square, a tiny device with accompanying app for iOS and Android smartphones and tablets. It's ridiculously simple: Sign up for a Square account at www.squareup.com, and they'll mail you for free a tiny swiper device that plugs into your phone's headphone jack. (Or you can buy one at an Apple store for about $10, and it comes with a $10 rebate card.) Confirm your identity with your bank information, and you're ready to start accepting payments. The fees are just 2.75% of each swipe. Easy peasy!

Other alternatives

If you're not based in the US , you may have to figure out other ways to receive payment, as PayPal doesn't support transactions in some countries. Jesse Breytenbach is a crafter in South Africa who uses Setcom (www.setcom.com), a service similar to PayPal. "It's a bit frustrating, as there are several online marketplaces that I'd love to join, but they aren't set up to deal with anything other than PayPal or checks. Accepting checks in foreign currency incurs such huge fees that it's not worth it for me," she says. "From local buyers, I accept payment simply via direct deposit into my bank account. I prefer not to accept cash. Using my bank account means there's a paper trail that makes my accounting much easier."

For accepting credit card payments at craft shows and through your own website, ProPay (www.propay.com) is a popular option for crafters. Various account options let you accept payments via smartphone, mobile web, phone or card reader. Google Checkout (checkout.google.com) is another popular way to process web payments. You pay 30 cents per transaction plus 2.9 percent of the sale price.

Bookkeeping

A lot of the crafters I talked to use QuickBooks (quickbooks.intuit.com) for their bookkeeping, and many file their own taxes. Holly Klump is a sole proprietor, so her business income is all personal income. "I like being in complete control of my business," she says. "Whatever I do and whatever I put into it is how much I get out of it. It's pretty straightforward that way. If I move, I can move the business with me."

Kati Hanimägi uses QuickBooks for all of her invoicing, banking and credit card ledgers. "I would be lost without it," she says. Willo O'Brien uses QuickBooks, which integrates with Stitch Labs, a tool from a company she cofounded. Stitch (www.stitchlabs.com) can be used for contact management, inventory management, tracking income and orders—stitching together all your online and offline sales.

Breytenbach has enlisted the help of a tax consultant ever since an expensive snafu. "One year I forgot to fill in one of the boxes, and the department of revenue asked me for a vast amount of money! I paid it, but then one of my friends recommended their tax consultant. He found the error and got the money back for me. Since then, I've used him," she says. "He receives all my tax documents, makes sure they're filled in correctly and files them for me. I provide him with all my figures, income and expenses. It really helps, knowing that someone else is going to have to make sense of my columns of figures. I keep everything as orderly as I can, to make his job simpler (and faster—he charges by the hour) and so that I can answer any questions he might have easily."

Think you'll need a little help come tax time? Lauren Bacon suggests asking for recommendations from local small business associations. "Word of mouth finds these people best," she says. "Work-at-home bookkeepers can be a good asset—they may be into bartering. And a good bookkeeper will always know a good accountant."

I found an accountant for my craft show business by searching on LinkedIn (www.linkedin.com) for CPAs in the Cincinnati area who had experience with creative businesses. When I found one who'd done work for a yoga instructor and an artist, I contacted her via LinkedIn, and we've worked together ever since. When you find an accountant, don't be ashamed to ask for help setting up your bookkeeping software!

The New Tax Form: 1099-K

In 2011, the IRS introduced a tax form to report Internet income, the 1099-K. If you received payments in excess of $20,000 and more than 200 transactions in a given year, you'll receive a 1099-K from the payment processor (such as PayPal). Then you report the amount on the 1099-K in your gross income on your tax return. For more help, go to www.irs.gov.

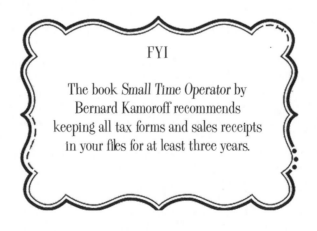

FYI

The book *Small Time Operator* by Bernard Kamoroff recommends keeping all tax forms and sales receipts in your files for at least three years.

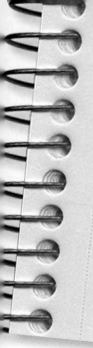

Lauren Bacon on . . .
Accountants vs. Bookkeepers

"A bookkeeper is someone who helps keep your financials up-to-date and your paperwork in order, tracking income and expenses. An accountant is like a lawyer in that they want to know about assets, liabilities, balance sheets, the status of your business—big-picture things. They aren't going to care how much you spent on taking a client out to dinner, but the bookkeeper will pay attention to that. For my business, we didn't get an accountant until we incorporated. Part of that is because we could do our taxes ourselves, and an accountant's hourly rate is often three figures. You could do your books yourself and then go to an accountant to file.

"A bookkeeper can help you set up accounting software, teach you how to use it and chat a few times a year to make sure you're on track. We talk to the bookkeeper when we have a weird expense or an unpaid bill and aren't sure how to record it. We also call on her for random things, like double-checking our payroll calculations and keeping track of the depreciation of our assets. A bookkeeper's a really valuable person to have around."

KEEPING IT LEGAL

If you're going to be all official, there are a few different forms your business can take:

- Sole proprietorship
- Limited partnership
- Limited liability company
- Corporation

Anybody starting a business is automatically a sole proprietor, so that's the business form most of my advice focuses on. When you're a sole proprietor, all the business income is part of your personal income. (And if someone sues your business, they're suing you—the more complicated business forms offer more protection of your personal assets.)

Getting business advice

Now, I'm no lawyer, so please carry out your due diligence with a business adviser, or at least devour some books about running a small business, like *Small Time Operator* by Bernard Kamoroff, which many of the crafter-slash-business-owners I talked to recommended. Check out the offerings for entrepreneurs in your area—local colleges, chambers of commerce or libraries often offer small business classes for free or very cheap.

Holly Klump found a microbusiness development class in her town that got her started. "It was meant for lower-income people trying to start small businesses," she says. "You were hooked up with a business advisor, and it was a nine-month program where they walked you through creating a business plan and helped you figure out your goals." The business plan part was largely focused on people seeking loans for their business—which Klump wasn't—but part of it was about saving money. "My program would double-match you up to a certain amount you saved—if you saved $500, you'd get $1,500. You drew out what you'd spend the money on, and they cut you a check. That's when I registered my business name, had a website designed and bought supplies."

Klump found that meeting regularly with her business adviser helped keep her focused and motivated amid many distractions. "I was also finishing my bachelor's degree and working at the time," she says. After registering her business name, she got a tax ID number to be able to write off business expenses and buy wholesale. "Plus, being legal protects you. You can't be making money on the side and not report it," she says. "As much as I'd like to just take my money and run, I think it's better to do things the legal way because you never know what can come back to bite you."

Anyone in the US can get a tax ID number (called an employer identification number or EIN) for free for business use at www.irs.gov/businesses. You'll need it to open up a business checking account, file to be an LLC, and numerous other biz tasks. But it also serves as a substitute for your SSN if you're a sole proprietor—that way you don't have to give out your social to everybody you do business with.

Lauren Bacon agrees. "Always file your taxes and keep receipts. If your goal is to make money and be compensated fairly, you want to track that for your own sake," she says. "If you're a cash-based business, you're on the honor system with the government."

Getting legal advice

If you decide to incorporate your business or need help with contracts or copyright issues, you want the help of a lawyer. Susie Ghahremani of boygirlparty has sought legal assistance for trademark and copyright infringement problems. "Since I'm an artist, I've had to defend and protect my artwork from misuse and imitation," she says. "I've also worked on contract negotiations with lawyers, who understand the terminology of contracts and agreements better than I ever will."

Bacon recommends looking for someone who's a litigating lawyer. "Some lawyers never go near the court," she says. "If you've got a great style and need to watch for people infringing on it, it's a real benefit to you to have a litigating copyright lawyer on your side. You have to find someone who's a bit of a shark."

Not sure where to find a lawyer? Bacon suggests three routes:

- Ask other crafters who they work with. "Go to networking events for crafters and anyone who's in a similar kind of business," she says. "You have to find someone you can trust, who can protect you, who's smart and understands a little about your industry and what you want. If they're used to dealing with megacorps, they're not even going to understand the concept of your biz."

- Contact professional associations for lawyers. "The staff can give recommendations of people to call," she says. "It's going to be different depending on what you need—incorporating and intellectual property/copyright issues might require two different lawyers. Or it might not."

- Ask your hairdresser. "They might not know the best lawyer, but they'll know the best gossip about them."

When you find some possible candidates for your BLF (best lawyer forever), do your homework before your first meeting: Read up on the legalities of what you're doing so you can ask good questions. "Meet with a few people and ask them pointed questions about the stuff you've learned, with concrete examples from your business," Bacon advises. "That'll test their knowledge and gauge how respectful they are with you. Lawyers have a crazy-high hourly rate, so you want to know you're getting your money's worth."

A lawyer's job is to help you assess legal risks and watch out for pitfalls. If they're worth their salt, they'll ask you lots of questions about your business and where you're going. Ask about their background, who their other clients are and what their primary areas of expertise are. Then describe the kind of legal advice you need, and ask explicitly if those are services they provide. If you're on the fence, ask for references. "I do that all the time. If I'm moving into a building, I ask to talk to another tenant and ask them about the landlord," Bacon says.

"An ideal situation for an indie crafter is to find a lawyer who will give a discounted rate in return for some other concession, such as correspondence via e-mail rather than meeting in person, with a turnaround time of a few days for responses," she says. "Ask the lawyer straight up: 'What's the most effective use of the time I pay you for?' The nice thing about lawyers is that they work insanely efficiently. So gather together all your queries at once. Lawyers teach us a valuable lesson about efficiency. I'll be like, 'We have 13 agenda items and 15 minutes to get through them all. Let's go!'"

Generally, lawyers will give you itemized invoices if they're on a monthly retainer; you'll pay for things such as couriers, long-distance charges and travel costs—all of which is spelled out in the contract you and the lawyer agree on at the beginning of your relationship. If you don't have the lawyer on retainer, you'll just get a bill upon completion of the project.

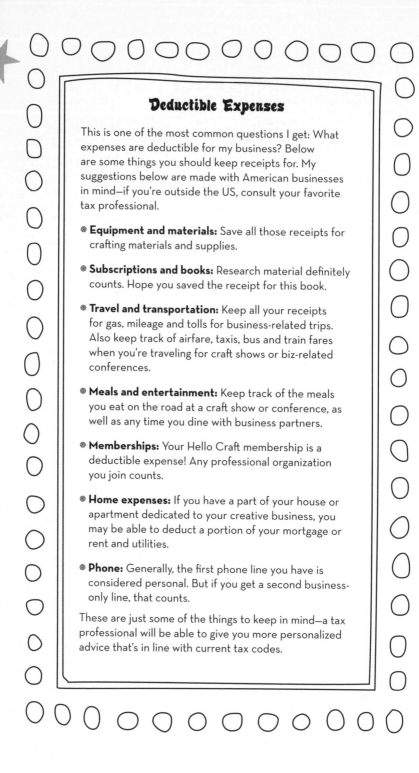

Deductible Expenses

This is one of the most common questions I get: What expenses are deductible for my business? Below are some things you should keep receipts for. My suggestions below are made with American businesses in mind—if you're outside the US, consult your favorite tax professional.

⦿ **Equipment and materials:** Save all those receipts for crafting materials and supplies.

⦿ **Subscriptions and books:** Research material definitely counts. Hope you saved the receipt for this book.

⦿ **Travel and transportation:** Keep all your receipts for gas, mileage and tolls for business-related trips. Also keep track of airfare, taxis, bus and train fares when you're traveling for craft shows or biz-related conferences.

⦿ **Meals and entertainment:** Keep track of the meals you eat on the road at a craft show or conference, as well as any time you dine with business partners.

⦿ **Memberships:** Your Hello Craft membership is a deductible expense! Any professional organization you join counts.

⦿ **Home expenses:** If you have a part of your house or apartment dedicated to your creative business, you may be able to deduct a portion of your mortgage or rent and utilities.

⦿ **Phone:** Generally, the first phone line you have is considered personal. But if you get a second business-only line, that counts.

These are just some of the things to keep in mind—a tax professional will be able to give you more personalized advice that's in line with current tax codes.

Jenny Hart on . . .
Dealing with Copycats

The Sublime Stitcher herself has dealt with some nasty knockoffs of her work. Generally, she recommends going straight to a lawyer when dealing with a corporate copycat and trying to resolve things crafter-to-crafter when it's a solo scofflaw.

"It's a very difficult situation to navigate. If a person feels that copyright infringement is going to be an issue for their business, I think it's a good idea to consult with a lawyer to see what steps should be taken in structuring your business (such as establishing copyrights, trademarks or patents), what type of language you may want to use to communicate your copyrights and how to pre-frame potential infringements.

"But, I also think it's wise to understand that most lawyers will look at any situation along the lines of worst case scenario and will lay out every possible action—which can be really scary to consider. But that's their job, and it's their responsibility to look at it that way. It's ultimately up to you to decide the best and most effective course of action."

SALES TAX CHEAT SHEET

If you're working with cash or just don't want to futz around with a calculator at your next show, get prepped by filling out a sales tax cheat sheet. Sales tax rates (and requirements for reporting) vary by local jurisdiction. Ask your tax preparer or accountant for advice on following local tax laws. If you don't know the local rate, you can look it up at www.zip2tax.com or just ask the show organizers. Five states have no sales tax: Alaska, Delaware, New Hampshire, Oregon and Montana.

City:

Local sales tax rate: ___%

Sale amount	Sale with tax
$1	_____
$2	_____
$5	_____
$10	_____
$15	_____
$20	_____
$25	_____
$30	_____
$40	_____
$50	_____

City:

Local sales tax rate: ___%

Sale amount	Sale with tax
$1	_____
$2	_____
$5	_____
$10	_____
$15	_____
$20	_____
$25	_____
$30	_____
$40	_____
$50	_____

City: _____

Local sales tax rate: ___%

Sale amount	Sale with tax
$1	_____
$2	_____
$5	_____
$10	_____
$15	_____
$20	_____
$25	_____
$30	_____
$40	_____
$50	_____

City: _____

Local sales tax rate: ___%

Sale amount	Sale with tax
$1	_____
$2	_____
$5	_____
$10	_____
$15	_____
$20	_____
$25	_____
$30	_____
$40	_____
$50	_____

City: _____

Local sales tax rate: ___%

Sale amount	Sale with tax
$1	_____
$2	_____
$5	_____
$10	_____
$15	_____
$20	_____
$25	_____
$30	_____
$40	_____
$50	_____

City: _____

Local sales tax rate: ___%

Sale amount	Sale with tax
$1	_____
$2	_____
$5	_____
$10	_____
$15	_____
$20	_____
$25	_____
$30	_____
$40	_____
$50	_____

Chapter 3

Selling Out

So you've figured out how much your plastic-canvas cupcakes are going to cost and found the perfect URL. But how are you going to get them into the hot little hands of the adoring public? You've got a lot of options.

The Internet helped fuel the indie craft revolution, so it's no surprise that so many handmade goods trade hands online. Selling through a site such as Etsy or through your own online storefront is a great entry point into craft commerce. But there are still IRL options. I'll show you how to get started placing your goods into brick-and-mortar shops on consignment or wholesale.

Whatever your sales strategy, you'll make good use of the tips on taking great photos, polishing your packaging and dealing with customers. Get ready to sell out!

WHERE TO SELL

One of the most awesome things about DIY business is the number of distribution options you have. No matter what you sell, how much you can produce or how good (or bad) you are with the Internet, you'll find an option that fits your needs.

Your own website

How it works: You build a website where people can buy stuff.

Costs involved: Quite a few, including domain registration, hosting fees, online payment processing fees and potentially a web designer if you aren't HTML literate.

Pluses: You are the master of your domain. The possibilities are endless!

Minuses: The initial setup costs a lot more than going with Etsy. It might be a headache if you want to be a crafter, not a webmaster. Plus, you have to let people know the site even exists.

Advice: If you're into DIY web design or have a roommate who dreams in HTML, go for it! Do link trades with other crafters and follow the promotion tips listed in Chapter 5. (For more on setting up a website, see page 60.)

Online consignment shops

How it works: You send in your stuff to the store organizers, set your prices and leave the selling up to them.

Costs involved: A portion of your selling price, plus shipping fees and your trust.

Pluses: It doesn't require a lot of maintenance and circumvents the traditional retail system.

Minuses: Because it's not exactly easy or lucrative to keep track of hundreds of $2 items, organizers sometimes flake out. There's also no guarantee that your items will sell.

Advice: Stick to established shops, or at least go with ones recommended by crafty friends.

Etsy

How it works: You create an online storefront for your brand and sell as many or as few of your crafts as you like.

Costs involved: Small listing fees and sales fees apply for every transaction. You also should consider the cost of shipping, though you can pass that on to the consumer.

Pluses: Thousands of shoppers browsing the site constantly, and there are built in promotional opportunities.

Minuses: Tens of thousands of items are for sale on Etsy, so it can be tough to stand out.

Advice: Having awesome pics is the first step to making a killing on Etsy. It's possible to pay extra to be a featured crafter. Get familiar with other crafters on the site, and star items and sellers that you like. Getting a mention on a major craft blog is a surefire way to sell out your store.

FYI

Etsy listings are active for three months. As time goes on, your listings move toward the end of the site's search results. When you renew your listings, you get back to the first page of results. So renew often!

Setting up Shop on Etsy

The anatomy of an Etsy storefront is pretty simple, but there are lots of little details to pay attention to. Here's the Etsy shop of Miss Chief Productions (misschief.etsy.com) as an example.

1   **Store banner:** An eye-catching banner that reflects your brand is important. It doesn't have to be complicated; in fact, less is often more. Follow the exact specifications for the image size you upload—you don't want the pic to be squished or stretched!

2   **Shop announcement:** Use this space to welcome visitors. Also make note of upcoming shows you're doing, if you're going to be unable to ship orders for a short time, recent press mentions and any other news.

3   **Featured listings:** Pick out three new or especially awesome items in your shop and give them top billing.

4   **Sections:** Creating sections lets shoppers browse by item type within your store. You can create up to 10 different sections under the Your Etsy>Shop Setup area.

5   **Item listings:** Make sure your individual listing titles are descriptive, but not so long that they get cut off.

Craft shows

How it works: You pay for table space and sell your brains out.

Costs involved: You pay an application and/or table fee, plus any travel costs and possibly a vendor's license and sales taxes.

Pluses: Selling at a show is great exposure, and it's an exciting atmosphere where you can meet buyers and other crafters.

Minuses: There's no guarantee of sales—or good weather. You also have to be prepared to be on your feet all day. Competition is tough to get into big shows.

Advice: Do it if you can afford to get to the venue. Go in with a friend if you're hesitant or want to split the expenses. See the next chapter for more advice on indie craft shows.

Brick-and-mortar stores

How it works: Many small shops buy work from individual artisans wholesale. You set your price—generally half of your retail price—and a store buys stuff from you to resell. Or they might host your work on a consignment basis, meaning they display and sell your work in exchange for keeping a percentage of the retail price.

Costs involved: Aside from the deep discount you have to offer, dealing with established stores will absolutely require you to stay straight with the IRS. You might also need to supply a retail display.

Pluses: The general public sees your stuff, and the shop's interest is a real endorsement for your work. You don't have to worry about dealing with the public.

Minuses: You'll bring in less cash than if you sold items yourself. Also, you rely on the store's reputation, and it's worth keeping in mind that many stores don't survive past their first year.

Advice: Scope out boutiques in your area and ask if they sell local designers' work. If it seems like a good match, arrange a short meeting to present your work, or give them your URL. Find out whether they prefer to buy wholesale or on consignment. It might be easier to get your work into a consignment-based store, since the risk for the shop is relatively low. If you're planning on pursuing wholesale, develop a price list to have on hand.

Kati Hanimägi on . . .
Selling Wholesale

Kati Hanimägi runs Oddball Press in Cleveland, Ohio.

"I began by creating a mailing list of about 500 specialty retailers—mostly stationery and gift stores. I created the list by researching different cities online, searching through shopping guides. If I felt the store might carry similar products, I added them to my list. I also asked friends and family for names of shops in their areas. Then I sent out my first catalog, introducing our line of 18 greeting cards. I sent card samples to 100 stores I thought had the most promise. I had the website up and ready, and basically crossed my fingers, hoping someone would order. I made the uncomfortable follow-up calls that everyone says you need to do, but I never got any orders from the cold phone calls. Since that first mailing, I've continued to send direct mail pieces that showcase new products. I'd recommend it to any crafter looking to break into the wholesale market.

"My biggest move to generate business in the wholesale market was to attend the National Stationery Show. It was a fantastic way to meet retailers, reps and fellow crafters. Our sales doubled, and we met many people. But it was a large expense between the booth, travel, being in New York City and other odds and ends. If you do a trade show, create a budget, stick to that budget, and come up with conservative sales projections."

Olivera Bratich on . . .
Approaching Shops

Olivera Bratich opened Wholly Craft in Columbus, Ohio, in 2005.

"Before approaching us, do a little homework. If you can, visit the shop in person to see if your items would be a good fit and if we carry anything similar already. If you're not in the area, read all the information offered on the website and check out other crafters we work with. This will give you a good idea of the context your work will be displayed and sold in, and how best to approach the shop.

"Approach a shop with a selection of your popular designs and pieces, not the stack of unsold items you have leftover from a craft fair. We have to make a decision on your entire line, so show your best work. If you're submitting work online for consignment consideration, invest a little time in learning to take good photos. And never get discouraged by rejection from any shop. Often it's not a direct reflection of your work. The shop may not be a good fit for your style or they might already carry something similar. In our case, our space is pretty limited, so at times we're not taking any new items in a particular category until we clear out what we have to make space."

Olivera Bratich stocks Wholly Craft with handmade paper goods, clothing, home decor, jewelry and more.

GET A WEBSITE

Even if you're planning on selling your wares exclusively through Etsy, wholesale orders or at craft shows, a website is one of the most valuable tools a crafter has for generating sales. Nobody will buy your decoupage candy bean earrings if they don't know you exist and have no way of finding you. Plus, it's helpful for people to know a little bit about you and your business before they commit to a purchase.

You don't need to be a web-design genius to get a site set up. One easy option is to register a free blog and redirect your own URL to it. (For more on blogging, see page 119.) You can do this by logging into the site where you registered your URL and creating a forward or redirect. You can integrate your Etsy and Flickr accounts with a blog very easily, and blog updates are a snap.

You can also try enlisting the help of an HTML-gifted pal to create a website. See if she's interested in exchanging services—say, she builds you a website you give her thirty plush octopi. It's a match made in heaven. Cinnamon Cooper of Poise.cc found a friend willing to do her website for free if she gave him free rein. (You can see the stunning results on the opposite page.) "Even if you don't know a web designer, look for a college student trying to build their portfolio," she suggests. "They'll ask questions you never considered—stuff like, 'What color is your business?' You learn how to explain and describe the feel of your business to someone who's creative but unconnected to it."

Regardless of which direction you go, your website absolutely must include these things:

- **Pictures of your crafts.** Even if you're not selling directly from your website, post lots of high-quality pictures (see the sidebar on page 64) and detailed descriptions. Organize your products by category, kind or theme so they're easy to browse.

- **Information about yourself.** Knowing something about the maker is what makes buying handmade so awesome. You don't need to share your entire life story or your full name; background information on how you started crafting, what you make and what inspires you will suffice.

Your website should show what you and your products are all about. Poise.cc's super-stylin' homepage flaunts Cinnamon Cooper's ethics as well as her wares. Bold links lead visitors further into the site, and there are no questions about Cooper's prices or policies.

> The designer will ask questions you never considered—stuff like, 'What color is your business?' You learn how to explain and describe the feel of your business.

—Cinnamon Cooper

- **Ordering policies.** For example, include where you sell your wares, how you accept payment, how quickly you ship and whether you accept returns. If you find people asking the same questions over and over, that's a good cue to add it to your FAQ.

- **How to contact you.** Include an e-mail address, a contact form and/or a business phone number. If you have a business mailing address or P.O. box, include that, but don't post your home address.

On a similar subject, your website must not under any circumstances contain:

- Eye-bleeding color combos
- Seizure-triggering flash graphics
- Slow-loading giganto photos instead of thumbnails (the Save for Web option in Photoshop should be your BFF)
- Blurry or washed-out photos
- Images of things you didn't make
- Text in cRaZy uPpEr-LoWeR-cAsE type

Susie Ghahremani's illustration style comes through on boygirlparty.com. The left column highlights her latest product, and the straightforward links make it easy for shoppers to find what they're looking for.

How to Make Your Own Light Box

Make your own light box to help you get those picture-perfect merchandise photos. All you need is a large sheet of white drawing paper, a stack of books and three desk lamps to get really professional-looking photos. (Note: This works best on smaller items.)

1 Make a stack of heavy books, about a foot high, on a table or desk. Get three desk lamps with bendy necks; use daylight or full-spectrum light bulbs to avoid giving your whites a yellow cast.

2 Put one end of the sheet of paper over the top of the stack of books; it should be big enough to cascade in front of the books and onto the desk, forming a mini stage. Don't crease or bend it—the paper will be your seamless background.

3 Put one lamp on top of the book stack to hold the paper in place and point the head toward the "stage" area. Place the other two lamps on the left and right sides of the stage area. Each bulb should be about a foot away from the object you're photographing; adjust the distances if necessary.

Now you're ready for your close-up!

Picture Perfect

The photos you post online are the first impression you make, so you've got to take the best pictures you can. (And featured sellers on Etsy always have really sweet photos.) The following photo tips are crafter-tested and author-approved.

1. Invest in a digital camera. You don't have to spend a fortune to get a quality camera—you can find one for less than $150 that does everything you need it to do. (I've been using Canon PowerShots for years.) Make sure it has macro settings for detail shots, and spring for the extra-large memory card.

2. Make 'em big. Set the resolution high—300 dpi and at least 1200 × 1600 pixels. You'll resize them for the web, but you need high-res images on hand in case *Super Glossy Magazine* comes calling.

3. Set the scene. Busy backgrounds are major buzzkills. Never take pictures of your wares against your bedspread or, even worse, your rec room's shag carpet. Plain backgrounds put all the focus where it should be: on your products.

4. Light it up. Natural light is always best, but using a light box is even better for capturing details. (See page 63 to learn how to make a DIY light box.) Never use a built-in flash for close-ups. It will wash out your image beyond recognition.

To show off her stenciled tea towels, Jesse Breytenbach shot them in a staged setting using natural light.

A close-up shot—like this one of Breytenbach's tea towels—shows off details that make your product stand out as well as show off your craftsmanship.

5. **Take four.** Design*Sponge's Grace Bonney recommends crafters get four pictures of every item: a close-up shot, a full shot, a situation shot and a shot that shows how your product is unique, like that Bolivian chain stitch your nana taught you. Use the macro setting on your camera to get the close-ups. If you're within 8" (21cm) of the product, it's the only way to keep the image crisp.

6. **Polish up.** You don't need Photoshop to make your photos awesome—there are plenty of cheap or free options out there, such as Photoshop Effects, the open source GIMP and the online Picnik (which is integrated with Flickr). If you lack mad Photoshop skills, just use the AutoCorrect color and brightness/contrast features to fix up your photos. Skip the sharpness options, though. If your original image is fuzzy, artificially sharpening it will look wack.

7. **Save it all.** Create a naming system that makes it easy to figure out exactly which pictures are which. Use something like 2012-redteacozy-300dpi.jpg instead of the default DSC01028.jpg. While you're at it, save a smaller 72dpi version, too. Back up your photos periodically by burning them onto CDs, saving them on an external hard drive or uploading them to an online storage system. It seems like a hassle—but only until it's coulda-woulda-shoulda time.

Presentation

It's all about first impressions. If you mail off your handmade soap in a sandwich bag filled with glitter, all you're going to do is tick off your customers (and possibly cause major skin irritation). When you start selling, you have to create a consistent look for your crafts.

When it comes to packaging, you might only need something as simple as a tag for your soft goods, or you might need a sturdy sheath that can double as a mailer. Where you're selling also determines to some extent the wrapping you require. A simple wrapper might suffice for an Etsy sale, but if you want to sell wholesale to boutiques, you need something that's eye-catching and can stand on its own.

I love packaging that's elegant and simple. Your package could be as simple as using a custom-printed wide rubber band to hold together a stack of hand-printed cards. The main thing is to create a look for your crafts' packaging that accurately represents your style and motivations. (You can find great examples of packaging at www.flickr.com/groups/etsypackaging.) When you come up with a look you like, invest in bulk orders of bags, mailers, stickers and other supplies from eBay or wholesale retailers to keep your per-item cost low.

Remember that packaging also has to protect your goods, not just look pretty. Jenny Harada, who makes plush creatures, uses the free priority boxes from the post office. "I put all my items in plastic zip bags in case the package gets wet," she says. "I bought a bunch of large zip bags from a wholesale supply place. It's so worth it to keep the goods intact and bundled together so they don't fall out all over the place when the box is opened."

When you ship off an order, add a personal message that lets the customer know you appreciate their business and reminds them there's a real person behind the product. I like to write a little thank-you note on a cool piece of vintage paper.

Jesse Breytenbach's brooches are wrapped in a scored kraft tag, which is stamped and fastened with ribbon.

Mix-and-Match
Packaging Concepts

Choose one (or two) items from each container to come up with a packaging
concept that works best for you.

Basic Package

- cardboard box
- shoebox
- envelope
- cloth bag
- lunch bag
- paper grocery bag
- gift box
- butcher paper
- scored fold-over mailer

- poly bag
- takeout box
- poster tube
- glass jar
- static-proof bag
- glassine paper envelope
- paper coffee cup
- burlap sack
- reusable tote bag
- mesh pouch

Modifiers

- screen printing
- spray painted stencils
- collaged cutouts
- colored vinyl or duct tape
- stitching
- stamps
- personalized stickers
- stapled labels
- decorative tape
- string
- wide rubber band
- ribbon

Padding

- tissue paper
- fabric scraps
- newsprint
- vintage sewing patterns
- shredded junk mail
- bubble wrap
- foam sheets
- kraft paper
- fake grass

Customer service

The orders are rolling in! How do the crafty superstars keep track of it all?

Some crafters keep Excel databases of all their orders; others put the info on index cards and attach them to baskets to fill with the orders. No matter your system, keeping your workspace in order will help you fulfill orders quickly. (You can use the forms in the appendix on pages 186–187 to help keep track of your orders.)

Personally, I fill orders as I get them through Etsy and PayPal. Susie Ghahremani goes the Excel route. "As a sole proprietor, I don't need anything fancy, just a database and a well-labeled filing system for papers and receipts," she says.

If any issues arise between when the buyer places an order and receives it, communicate with them any issues promptly and plainly. Be straightforward—no excuses. State on your website or in your Etsy shop what days you normally ship items and how long order fulfillment will take.

"In the best of bad situations, a talk can help clear up giant misunderstandings," Ghahremani says. "One of the perks of being a small, crafty business is that pretty much everyone you work with has a name, a face, a personality and is real, unlike faceless gigantic corporations. So talking things out is a very real solution to problems."

Faythe Levine tries to answer all e-mails within a day. "If I get an e-mail and I don't respond right away, I know it's gonna be at least a week until I get back to it," she says.

Crafters love to share information and experiences, but what if someone's getting a little too nosy? When people ask Hannah Howard of Lizzie Sweet how she makes her bath and beauty products, she jokes, "I'd tell you, but I'd have to kill you. I'm like, 'Dude, there's a price tag on it. I'd tell you, but not without you paying me something for it.'" Humor is the great deflector.

Customer service scenario guide

Every crafter is bound to run into a problem sooner or later. Learn how to deal with some common issues with this scenario guide with commentary from Jessica Manack of Miss Chief Productions.

Scenario #1: A customer says they paid, but you never got the money.

What to do: First off, confirm all the information—did the customer send the payment to the right address or the correct PayPal account? Ask for a proof of payment. Manack advises that you state on your website that items ship upon receipt of payment or check clearance. "Clearly lay out which kinds of payment you prefer. PayPal is a really safe way of accepting payments—money orders and cash can just get taken from the mail. If someone sends a check, send them a confirmation e-mail to let them know when you get it," she says. "When I get an order, I let the customer know when I'll ship the order and via which service." Being overly communicative is a good way to prevent customers from getting frustrated. And never send out an order without getting the cash in hand. You'll find it's a lot harder to track down payments after the customer's already got the items.

Lesson learned: Using an online payment system like PayPal takes the responsibility of payment processing off your hands.

Scenario #2: The customer never received an order.

What to do: Check all your records to be absolutely sure you sent the package to the correct address and also make sure that it isn't crammed in your messenger bag or under the seat of your car. My policy is to respond right away, telling the customer what date I sent the package, via which shipping service and apologize for the delay. Ask the customer to let you know if the merchandise hasn't arrived in a week, and follow up if he or she doesn't get back to you.

Sometimes the mail is just delayed and the problem resolves itself, but sometimes your package disappears into some crafty Bermuda Triangle. If this is the case, I usually offer to send a replacement at my own cost and ask the buyer to return one item if both eventually show up. If the item was one-of-a-kind, offer a replacement or store credit. Manack suggests working delivery confirmation into your shipping fees if your products are pricey. You can also state in your shop that you offer delivery confirmation and insurance, but at an added cost. If you're shipping internationally, things can get caught up in customs, causing delays. Within the US, you can verify addresses at www.usps.com. Manack always gets the ZIP+4 for addresses. "I've heard that if you add that, it makes your shipping faster, and it's also a way to double-check the address," she says. It doesn't hurt to compare an Etsy address with the PayPal address, too.

Lesson learned: Consider springing for delivery confirmation and insurance, and always double-check mailing addresses.

Scenario #3: A hater starts bad-mouthing your biz online.

What to do: Anybody who's reached a moderate level of success has encountered somebody like this. Maybe bittergirl89 is leaving nasty feedback or is trolling around your favorite message board with mean-spirited responses to you. Generally, there's not a lot to be done in regard to haters, aside from ignoring them.

"Don't get caught up in it," Manack says. "Correct misinformation politely, and feedback helps keep people in line. Feedback helps customers make good decisions, and it makes you seem more transparent." If the person crosses the line of defaming your business and tarnishing your character, it might be worth it to trace the person's IP address and contact the Internet service provider to let them know about their customer's breach of service.

Lesson learned: Rise above the hate.

// Feedback helps customers make good decisions, and it makes you seem more transparent. *//*

—Jessica Manack

Scenario #4: You've received a large order from Nigeria.

What to do: It seems unlikely, but even artists and crafters are targets for e-mail scams. Often the e-mail expressing interest in your wares will be vague, without mentioning specific items. Sometimes the person purports to be a shop owner who'd like to carry your wares. Other times the person says he's traveling and needs you to ship to an intermediary, and he offers to cut you a check for a lot more cash for the inconvenience. The bottom line: Never accept overpayments or give out your bank account information, and avoid using wire services for any transaction. If you think the customer is legit, wait to ship your goods until you have the money in your hand—international transfers or money orders can take a week or two to clear.

Lesson learned: If it sounds too good to be true, it probably is.

Scenario #5: Somebody is selling a blatant copy of one of your crafts.

What to do: First, take a breath and get some perspective. Ask a friend if you're overreacting before you take your case to Judge Judy. It might only take a conversation with your competitor to straighten things out. But if you can't reach an acceptable resolution, consider taking legal action. This kind of scenario is a good argument for filing copyrights. What if the perpetrator isn't some punk with an Etsy shop but rather a corporation that copped your style? A terse e-mail isn't likely to do much. Find a lawyer who specializes in intellectual property and copyright.

Lesson learned: Consider copyrighting your work.

HOW TO NOT SELL

The awesome thing about being in an alternative economy like crafting is that you can set your own rules. Maybe you're OK with just breaking even, perhaps you want to use your business to support charitable causes, or maybe you just want to create stuff to trade with other artisans.

Trades are a long-standing tradition in the creative communities. I love doing them—after my hairstylist found out I was a bookbinder, we did an exchange: I made her a journal to her specifications, and she gave me a haircut. Score! I first got in touch with crafter Jesse Breytenbach through a printed fabric swap. Crafty message boards often will have an area devoted to trades, which is a really fun way to make use of pieces you don't intend to sell.

Lauren Bacon, co-author of *The Boss of You*, has a very fashionable trade agreement between her web design company and a local clothing designer. "We update her site every spring and fall with her new collections," Bacon says. "We track our time and then go to her store and get the amount of clothes that corresponds with the value of the time we spent working on her site." But Bacon also warns that you shouldn't trade with just anybody. If you don't really need $200 worth of bedazzled eye masks, just say no! "If you weren't intending to be a charity, it can be not very fun," she says.

Cinnamon Cooper started Poise.cc giving half the cost of her bags to women-focused charities, but she realized that with the costs of running a business and buying fabric, she was losing money. "It was fine at first, but after I got to the point where I wanted to make it sustainable, I realized that making enough money to pay off my credit card purchases would be a good thing," she says. Now, just select bags are associated with nonprofits, with about 20 percent of her sales going to charity. If you donate your goods to a registered nonprofit, get receipts so you can use the deduction on your taxes.

Hannah Howard on . . .
Bartering

"The guy who drew the Lizzie Sweet girl [below] did it for a scarf. I rely on contracts—if I'm going to do something for someone, I make sure I have it in writing and that we agree on the terms. It just keeps everybody in the clear. Contracts can make people nervous sometimes, but it's not that the other person doesn't think you're honest, it just gets you on the same page. I got a contract template off the Internet and altered it for my barters. Sometimes an e-mail conversation with the details is enough, but if it's not in writing, it can be kind of mercurial."

Chapter 4

Indie Craft Shows

The first thing "craft show" conjures up in most people's minds is a junior high gymnasium affair with vendors hawking starched doilies, garish tole paintings and lawn geese attire. My own first venture into craft commerce was at a show in a church basement. The table fee was less than $20—but so was my total revenue for the day.

Thankfully, the indie craft show came along. In the last decade, the number of shows catering to alternative crafts has exploded, so the unorthodox crafter has boundless opportunities, from a couple card tables set up in a café to truckzilla-size shows. Sales can be good or bad, but every show is still a promotional opportunity. If there aren't any indie craft shows in your area, consider starting one of your own! It takes some work, but you can do it on the cheap and help cultivate a craft community in your own town.

Quiz: What Kind of Crafter Are You?

You don't need to be the next Jenny Hart to clean up at a craft show, but you should have your little ceramic pirate ducks in a row. The results of this quiz will give you tailored suggestions for taking on the indie craft show circuit.

1. Are you already selling your stuff online or in shops?
   a. Here's my URL and my publicist's number.
   b. I've been thinking about it.
   c. Why would I? My grandma buys me out before anyone else can.
   d. Yeah, on Etsy!

2. Does your business have a name?
   a. Yes, and a trademarked logo and a spin-off brand for kids.
   b. Not really.
   c. Kat's Kountry Krafts
   d. I just came up with one: Glittercraft Flutterbuy!

3. Have you spent much time developing and perfecting your crafts?
   a. Well, yeah—otherwise I wouldn't have gotten that shoutout in *BUST*.
   b. I feel most secure when covered in glue.
   c. I've got toilet paper cozies down to a science.
   d. I do most of my crafting at my weekly Stitch 'n Bitch.

4. How would you describe your style/aesthetic?
   a. Sleek, chic and cheeky.
   b. Quirky, dark and entirely indie.
   c. Potholders only my grandma could love.
   d. Sparkly, fluffy and fun!

5. What words would you use to describe yourself?
   a. Confident, outgoing, ambitious.
   b. Shy, moody, introverted.
   c. Traditional, cautious, kitschy.
   d. Friendly, optimistic, happy-go-lucky.

6. Have you ever been to a craft show?
   a. I hit up Renegade and Bazaar Bizarre every year.
   b. I prefer not to go outside.
   c. I hit up every craft show/bake sale in the tri-county area.
   d. I sell at a local indie trunk show.

7. How do you feel about crunching numbers in your head?
   a. No problem—I was a mathlete.
   b. I am incapable of making change.
   c. Why do I need to crunch them?
   d. That's what calculators are for.

8. Do you like interacting with the public?
   a. I know how to rope them in and make the sale.
   b. I told you before—I prefer not to go outside.
   c. I love trading plastic canvas tips.
   d. I am all about meeting other crafters.

9. What's your ideal craft show location?
   a. Anywhere I can go with my frequent flier miles.
   b. My own apartment.
   c. A church basement or high school gym.
   d. Anything within driving distance.

10. What do you want to get out of your craft show experience?
    a. Achieve total craft domination.
    b. Not have any panic attacks . . . and sell some stuff.
    c. Connect with other proponents of traditional macramé.
    d. Meet other crafters, make some money and have fun!

Turn the page to find out your quiz results!

Quiz Results

How'd you score?

Mostly A: Biz Maven

Your mad craft skills are paralleled only by your ability to juggle invoices, inventory and iChat while blogging about your latest batch of vendibles. But for as much as you've got it going on in the business department, you could use some extra pointers on how to really flex your craft connections. Pay special attention to the advice in this chapter on etiquette. And if your town doesn't have a show, check out the section on starting your own, you overachiever.

Mostly B: Craft Hermit

No crafter is an island. You are a whiz with a Dremel, but when your only social outlet is Craftster, isolation is likely to dull the shine on your sequins. Make a day trip to scope out the nearest craft show, bring your Paxil and a pen, and I promise you'll be inspired—you might even make a few friends. Read up on customer service and craft show etiquette, and you'll be ready to sell!

Mostly C: Old-School Crafter

I'm going to be honest with you—indie craft show organizers are very discerning. It might sound a little elitist, but if you don't fit the aesthetic of a DIY show, you aren't going to get accepted. Irony is totally welcome, but all signs are pointing toward you being really serious about those plastic canvas bookmarks. Check out the scene at your closest indie craft show before you apply to sell at one.

Mostly D: DIY Butterfly

You are all about collaborating with other crafters and don't shy away from your potentially adoring public. Your enthusiasm will go far in making sure you have a good time at a craft show, but you gotta check yourself before you wreck yourself. Don't promise more than you can deliver, and pay extra attention to the business side of things before your first show. Consider sharing a table with a friend!

ARE YOU READY?

Whether she's an old hand or dipping her toes in the craft show kiddie pool for the first time, every crafter has to pick her battles. There are just so many good shows these days that it'd be impossible to hit up every one of them without a legion of employees.

First, check your quiz results on the previous page to determine your crafty fortitude. Consider these things before you start applying to every show that looks cool: your prior craft show experience, how much stock you'd have by the show date and, most importantly, whether you can afford it. The monster shows can cost upwards of $100 a day to display, but small, local shows are often very affordable. Do some rough calculations with the craft show profitability worksheet on page 87 to get an idea of whether you'd break even at a show you have to travel to.

I love craft shows in unique spaces, like when Craftin' Outlaws was in an old church-turned-arts center in Columbus, Ohio.

APPLICATION PROCESS

Most of the big craft shows are juried, which means the organizers decide who makes the cut based on an application. The competition is stiff—some shows have acceptance rates rivaling those of Ivy League colleges.

Application

Organizers have a lot of things to consider when choosing who sells at their fair. Is there a good balance of different kinds of crafts? (Jewelry is notoriously over-represented in most application pools, for example.) Is a crafter doing something really unique? Some shows set aside a certain number of tables for newbies each year. Others really love focusing on local talent, like Chicago's DIY Trunk Show, run by the Chicago Craft Mafia. Poise.cc's Cinnamon Cooper, one of the judges, says they don't accept anyone farther than five hours away from Chicago, and about 80 percent of their sellers are in Chicago or its suburbs. "Part of it's logistical," she says. With Chicago's wonderful winter weather, "people coming in from Ohio and Kentucky have had problems and bailed out of the one-day show." Cooper says they also try to keep about 10 to 15 percent of their tables open for newbies, because she and partner Amy Carlton were very green when they started the show.

If you're new to the craft show scene, consider sharing a table with a friend. It can boost your chances of getting in because it's less of a risk for organizers to have two new crafters share a table than to give an entire space to someone who's never sold at a show before. Plus, it boosts the overall diversity of the show. Remember how I said there's always an overflow of jewelry peddlers? If you sell Shrinky-Dink earrings and your friend sells wallets woven from grocery bags, go in on an application together!

Liz Rosino, who started Craftin' Outlaws in Columbus, Ohio, has developed a precise process for selecting crafters. "After the deadline, all the complete applications are sorted into categories, such as jewelry, handbags and paper goods," she says. "It's really important to me to have a large variety of types of items—there are only so many booths for jewelry or bags. Those are probably the most popular categories, so they're the hardest to get a spot in. We even divide it down to people who make beaded jewelry, silver jewelry and so on, to make sure we have no duplicates."

Cooper says she looks for people using unique materials with a special focus on sustainability—economic as well as ecological. "We give extra points to recycled or fair trade items, and look for people who are being paid fair wages," she says.

If you really want to get into a show, the most important thing is to follow application instructions to a T, be on time and send photos that really do justice to your work. (See the tips on taking awesome photos on page 64.) Also make sure to read the application FAQ before e-mailing the show organizers—most of the time, all the answers you need will be on their website.

Rejection

Got turned down by your dream show? Don't get discouraged. Some big shows get more than four times the number of applications they can accept. That means the judging committee has to reject some damn good crafters. Kristen Rask, who runs the sweet store Schmancy in Seattle and works with the Urban Craft Uprising show there, has one common explanation for rejections: "People don't follow directions!" she says. "If you have 500 applicants or more, organizers get nitpicky."

So if the show organizers ask for attached photos, don't send a link. If you have to pay the table fee or an application fee when you apply, don't let yourself forget! (Table fees are generally returned to non-accepted crafters after the decisions have been made public; application fees are not returned. Whether there's a nonrefundable fee varies from show to show.)

If you do get the dreaded "thanks but no thanks" e-mail, be gracious. Rask has received some awkward post-rejection messages. "Sometimes people send e-mails saying, 'I'm really disappointed. This is the second year I've been rejected.' I feel bad, but that's no way to make me want to take you as a vendor!"

I've had some awkward encounters with crafters rejected from our show in Cincinnati. Crafty Supermarket gets more than 200 applications for just 50 spots, so we have to be very picky about who we accept, and we often have to reject really great makers. People who e-mail us post-rejection trying to get us to change our minds stand out—in a bad way.

Take heart in the fact that even big-time crafters and craft show organizers are rejected sometimes. Even though I run a show and wrote a book about craft business, I've heard plenty of nos, too. Understanding that there's a lot of competition and not taking the rejection personally is really important. Just keep perfecting your crafts and try again next time!

SHOW APPLICATION TRACKER

Download a spreadsheet version of this form at
store.marthapullen.com/crafty-superstar-ultimate-craft-business-guide.

Show Name	City	Show Date	Application Deadline

Cost	Applied?	Accepted?	Sales

GETTING PREPPED

Getting that first congratulatory e-mail from the craft show organizer is an exhilarating feeling. And now the real work starts!

Travel arrangements

Aside from tons of your crafts, a table display and other odds and ends, you also have to figure out your travel and lodging arrangements if it's not a local show. (See the craft show profitability worksheet on the next page to help you figure out what you can afford.) Often the organizers will send info on affordable lodging—some even try to match up crafters with local hosts or hotel roommates. It's a good idea to reach out to your Facebook friends to see if any wayward relatives or college buddies live in the area you're visiting. Check the list of crafters selling at the show to see if any live near you, and send them a friendly e-mail to see if they're interested in carpooling. If you've got to go it alone, check sites like Priceline (www.priceline.com) and Kayak (www.kayak.com) for airfare and hotel deals.

Jenny Harada on ...
Bringing Baby

Jenny Harada's kooky stuffed animals (and her babies) have made appearances at craft shows all across the country.

"Bring lots of snacks and toys and activities and a helper. Actually, I would recommend leaving them home if you can! In a way, it's fun to have them there, but it can also be stressful and distracting. If they are old enough to help out, it might be a different story, but I haven't reached that stage yet."

Craft Show Profitability

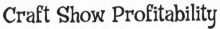

Is the craft show worth it? If you're looking to make big bucks and that's it, skip the show. If not, use the worksheet below to estimate how profitable a craft show will be for you. It will also help you track your real profits after attending a show.

EXPENSES

Application fee: _____

Table fee: _____

Vendor's license (if applicable): _____

Travel (gas, airfare, parking): _____

Lodging: _____

Food: _____

Other: _____

Total expenses: _____

Total expenses (B): _____

Total (anticipated) sales (A): _____

NET PROFIT (A – B): _____

Planning for the show

The show organizers will send you some basic information, such as when you should arrive on the day of the show to set up, anything special you need to bring (such as a tent if you'll be outside), and whether you need a local vendor's permit at the show. (But don't assume that if they don't say anything you're in the clear on sales tax. Check the state's department of taxation or revenue for all the rules.) Organizers are generally amazing, multitasking angels, but don't expect them to be able to hold your hand the entire time. Scour the show's website and devour all the vendor information you can find. You'll find that most FAQs are answered before you even ask.

If you plan to use a computer at the show, make sure there's Wi-Fi access for your laptop. Also, not all shows have electrical outlets for every booth. If you need juice, tell the organizers when you apply, or ask about it when table assignments are made.

If you're bringing a friend along, enlist them well ahead of time and make sure they've got all the info and know whether to request days off work. Having some extra hands is often really helpful, but make sure you compensate them for their time, whether it's in grub, hugs or real cash.

FYI

If your crafts are one of a kind, be sure to remove the items you take to the show from your online storefront. Etsy has an option to make items inactive. But make sure your store isn't completely empty! Many crafters report a jump in sales after a craft show.

TABLE DISPLAYS

First impressions are everything at a craft show. If your table is cluttered without a visible business name and no prices to be found, it's the aesthetic equivalent of bad BO.

If you've been to indie craft shows (if you haven't, you need to!), you know that the most popular sellers have the most eye-catching, pretty or unusual table displays. It doesn't take big bucks to make a great setup—all you need is a good imagination and a little planning.

Practice your setup on the kitchen table before you unveil it at a show. Ask a friend to give you feedback, and take pictures so you can replicate the layout on the day of the show.

It's key to think vertically. A table with everything laid out flat doesn't catch anyone's eye from across the room. Use shelves, boxes or stands to create height. Some sellers turn down the table and use room dividers or other completely vertical displays for their wares.

Assuming you're working with the common 8-foot folding table, the cornerstone of your display is the table covering. (Nobody wants to see all that scratched-up Masonite.) It should match your biz's look. Is your style utilitarian? Try plain kraft paper or corrugated cardboard. Is your style retro and hip? Go with a patterned bedsheet or curtains. Do you want to surprise visitors with something unusual? Get some Astroturf or bubble wrap! (Get more ideas on page 92.)

Go through your closets and kitchen with new eyes. What could you use for a display? Borrow your roommate's coat rack, clean off the dish rack, or use a stack of cool-looking books as props. Anne Holman displays her silver jewelry in white ceramic dishes. She uses a shallow white bowl filled with red lentils (see page 91) to show off her rings and flat sushi trays for her necklaces.

Kati Hanimägi of Oddball Press displays her letterpress cards and prints on top of stacks of prints that weren't up to snuff. "I knew that I wanted something very papery and utilitarian, so rather than use a tablecloth, I thought rolls of kraft paper would be the best neutral surface to make the product pop," she says. "From there, I drew up a simple little design for some wood racks that would hold three different card styles. I handed off the design to my handy husband, who built ten of them out of scrap wood we had piling up in the basement."

Then she just had to figure out how to set up the racks at different levels. "Originally, I covered hardback books with paper and stacked them up to get different heights for the racks to sit on. It looked good, but there was so much paper waste, and it was a lot of work to schlep around boxes of books." Hanimägi realized she could make use of 750 prints that weren't up to snuff. "I had a whole carton of printed chipboard with no use. As Craftin' Outlaws approached, I had the revelation to use the rejected prints as my risers. They're the most expensive risers I could have created, but I think they pull the booth together."

If you're lucky enough to live near an IKEA, spend a day scouring the Swedish superstore for cheap items you could repurpose to fit your needs. Thrift stores are also full of things you can turn into killer table displays. For example, I got some simple wooden CD crates for 50 cents each from Goodwill. I sanded them and coated them with silver spray paint to make them look flashy; they're the perfect size for displaying my hand-printed cards!

Aline Yamada of yumi yumi shows off her prints in simple wooden boxes from IKEA.

Some of Ann Holman's wares displayed on white
china under a bell jar

Anne Holman uses a shallow white bowl filled with
red lentils to show off her rings.

Creative Table Coverings

Choose one of these materials for an undoubtedly
awesome base for your table display.

Casual
gingham tablecloth

Quirky
Astroturf

Utilitarian
kraft paper

Earthy
burlap

Boho
printed cloth

Trendy
patterned fabric

Industrial
sheet metal

Green
old newspaper

Chic
pashmina

Rustic
barn wood

Homestyle
old quilt

Touchy
bubble wrap

Craft Show Booth Design Diagram

Sketch out ideas for your show table layouts on the next few pages. For tables, the most common size is 8' ×2.5' (2.5m × 0.75m), and booth spaces are usually 10' × 10' (3m × 3cm) or 12' × 12' (3.5m × 3.5m).

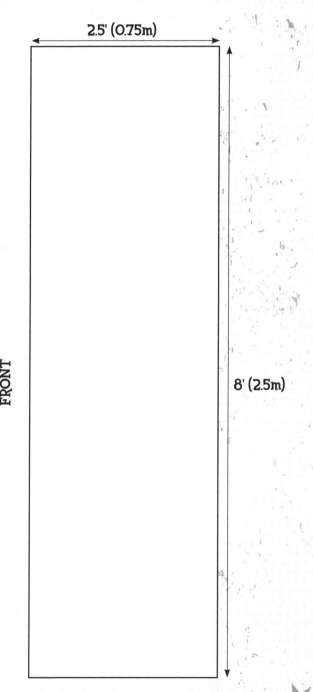

2.5' (0.75m)

FRONT

8' (2.5m)

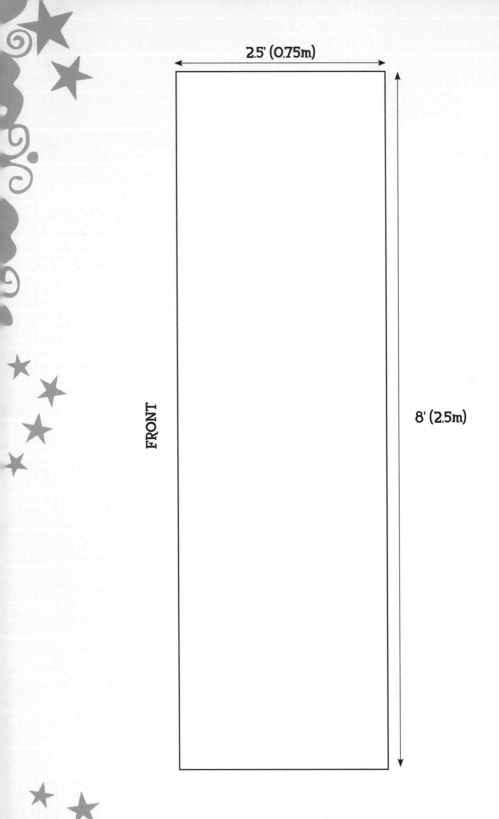

2.5' (0.75m)

8' (2.5m)

FRONT

2.5' (0.75m)

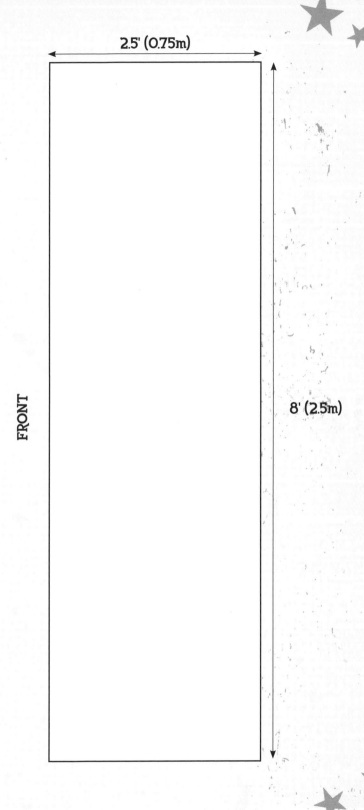

FRONT

8' (2.5m)

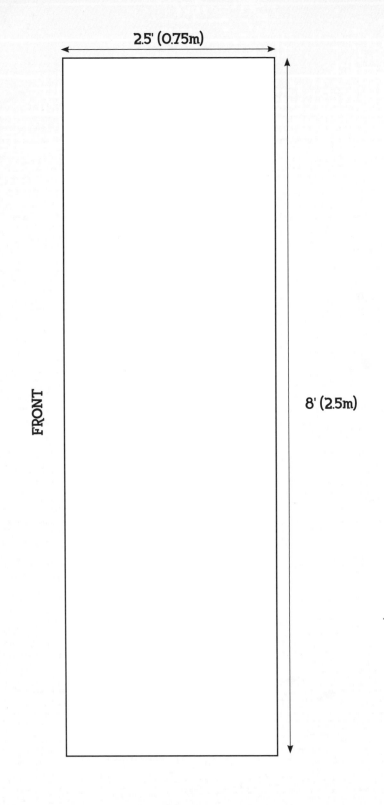

2.5' (0.75m)

8' (2.5m)

FRONT

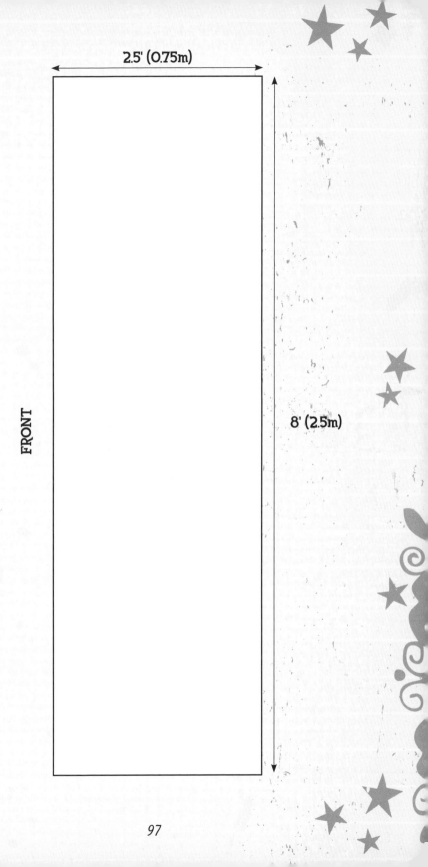

2.5' (0.75m)

8' (2.5m)

FRONT

10' (3m)

10' (3m)

FRONT

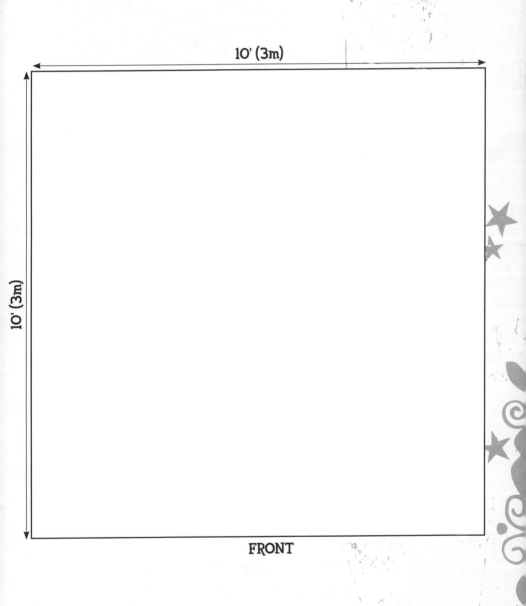

10' (3m)

10' (3m)

FRONT

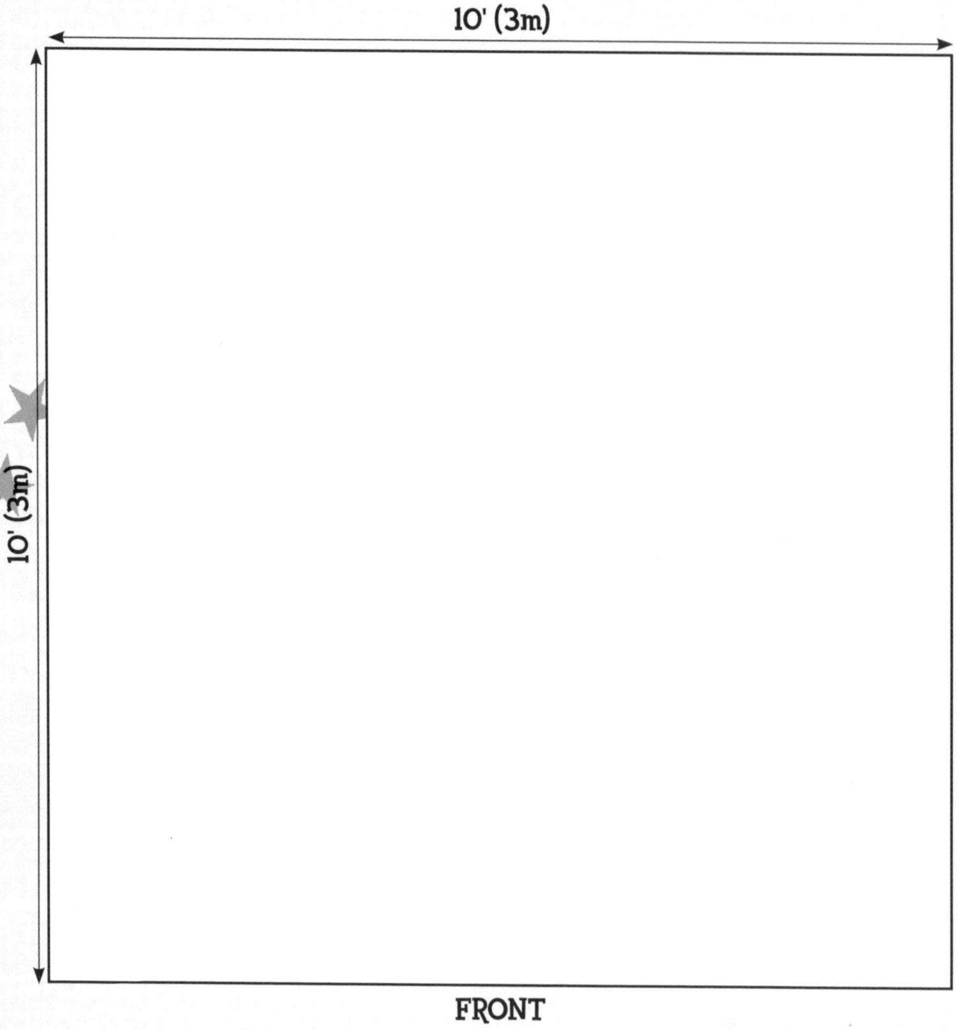

10' (3m)

10' (3m)

FRONT

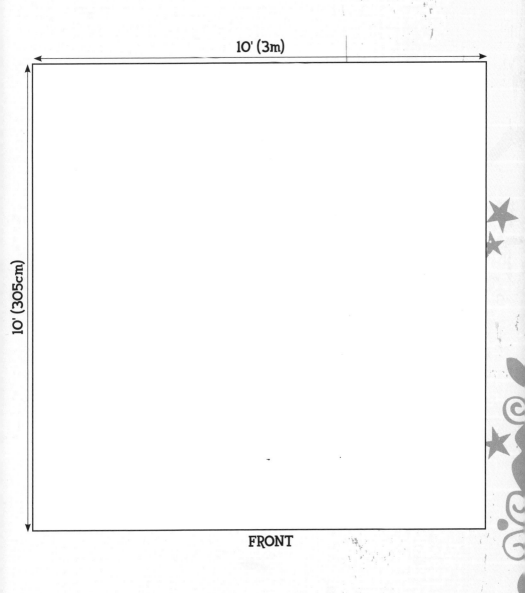

10' (3m)

10' (305cm)

FRONT

DAY OF SHOW

Rise and shine! Today's the big day, and as much as it might suck to be hauling your stuff around at 6 a.m., it's best to be on time or even early. After you get set up, you'll have time to relax, grab a bagel and meet your crafty neighbors.

If you're smart (and since you're reading this book, you obviously are), you'll have gotten everything together the night before the show and checked off everything on the list on page 104. I always make a grocery store trip and a bank run the day before a show to get snacks, drinks and change. (Get snacks that are easy to put down when a customer arrives—go for tidy bite-size things like crackers, grapes or granola bars. This is not the time or the place for hot wings.) Also do a quick inventory check the night before the show or before the doors open to make a record of how much stuff you brought with you.

You'll have your table setup down to a science by this point, so when you arrive at the show, you'll be able to check in and get started right away. Look for an organizer or volunteer when you arrive to get registered and find your table.

Introduce yourself to your crafty neighbors! I've met a lot of awesome people—and new friends—at indie craft shows. If nothing else, your tablemates will be the folks you turn to when you gotta make a restroom run. Most next-door neighbors are happy to watch your table for a sec if you offer to do the same.

FYI

One of the big upsides of traveling for shows is that you can build up your brand in other cities where people might not know your stuff. So, be sure everyone leaves your table with a sticker or business card with your name and URL on it.

Before you know it, the doors will open and you'll be flooded with curious customers! Don't be freaked about dealing with the public—people dig that they get to interact with crafters. Say hello to everyone who stops by your table, even if you doubt they'll buy anything. One great way to engage potential buyers is to share something about your technique. For example, when I see someone pick up a blank journal I made, I'll tell them the paper inside is all salvaged vintage stock. The most important thing is to stay friendly, even if your feet are killing you and you've been running all day on just a veggie dog. Standing behind your table makes you much more approachable than if you're sitting slouched with your arms crossed. Resist the temptation to work on your knitting when business is slow. Nothing says "I don't want to be here" more than a crafter paying more attention to her needles than her potential customers.

If you've got to collect sales tax, have a cheat sheet by your cash box for easy calculating. Having a calculator is handy, but why do the same multiplication dozens of times? Make sure everybody who buys from you signs up for your mailing list, which should be prominently displayed on your table on a clipboard with a functioning pen. Encourage everybody—even non-buyers—to take a sticker, business card or other freebie. Know where the nearest ATM is to be able to help cash-strapped shoppers. Some crafters don't take checks, but I generally do and haven't been burned yet. Ask to see the buyer's ID, and ask her to write her phone number on the check just in case. If you accept credit cards, always check the expiration date and for a signature on the back.

If you've got a friend with you to watch the table (or friendly neighbors), take time to walk around the show, meet other crafters and collect business cards. You can get a few new names for your blogroll, trade cross-stitching tips and make some friends while you're at it.

Though you might feel like you're running yourself ragged, take time to enjoy the ambience. Have you ever been surrounded by so many incredible, creative people in your life? This is enough to get me charged up and dancing behind my table even when I'm dog tired. If you're lucky, the show will have a DJ to keep you pumped the whole day.

Day-of-Show Checklist

FOR YOUR BOOTH

- ☐ more crafts than you think you'll need
- ☐ kickass table display
- ☐ sturdy totes, boxes or bags to transport your goods
- ☐ price tags and signs
- ☐ sign or banner with your business name
- ☐ business cards
- ☐ freebies (stickers, pins, fliers)
- ☐ e-mail sign-up list
- ☐ cash box
- ☐ table and chair if you have to supply your own
- ☐ tent if needed
- ☐ mirror if you're selling clothes, accessories or jewelry
- ☐ lighting if needed
- ☐ bags for customers (as simple as recycled grocery bags or as fancy as custom screen-printed paper bags)
- ☐ scissors, tape, pins
- ☐ pens, notebook, paper
- ☐ $50+ in small bills for change
- ☐ calculator
- ☐ your laptop or other credit card processing equipment
- ☐ book of sales receipts

FOR YOU

- ☐ water and other drinks
- ☐ layers of clothing
- ☐ sunscreen if you're outside
- ☐ aspirin, bandages, first-aid supplies and your regular meds
- ☐ snacks
- ☐ charged cell phone
- ☐ comfortable shoes
- ☐ wipes and/or antibacterial gel
- ☐ map and parking information
- ☐ some cash and a debit card for snacks and emergencies

Day-of-Show Checklist

FOR YOUR BOOTH

- [ ] more crafts than you think you'll need
- [ ] kickass table display
- [ ] sturdy totes, boxes or bags to transport your goods
- [ ] price tags and signs
- [ ] sign or banner with your business name
- [ ] business cards
- [ ] freebies (stickers, pins, fliers)
- [ ] e-mail sign-up list
- [ ] cash box
- [ ] table and chair if you have to supply your own
- [ ] tent if needed
- [ ] mirror if you're selling clothes, accessories or jewelry
- [ ] lighting if needed
- [ ] bags for customers (as simple as recycled grocery bags or as fancy as custom screen-printed paper bags)
- [ ] scissors, tape, pins
- [ ] pens, notebook, paper
- [ ] $50+ in small bills for change

- [ ] calculator
- [ ] your laptop or other credit card processing equipment
- [ ] book of sales receipts

FOR YOU

- [ ] water and other drinks
- [ ] layers of clothing
- [ ] sunscreen if you're outside
- [ ] aspirin, bandages, first-aid supplies and your regular meds
- [ ] snacks
- [ ] charged cell phone
- [ ] comfortable shoes
- [ ] wipes and/or antibacterial gel
- [ ] map and parking information
- [ ] some cash and a debit card for snacks and emergencies

Day-of-Show Checklist

FOR YOUR BOOTH

- [ ] more crafts than you think you'll need
- [ ] kickass table display
- [ ] sturdy totes, boxes or bags to transport your goods
- [ ] price tags and signs
- [ ] sign or banner with your business name
- [ ] business cards
- [ ] freebies (stickers, pins, fliers)
- [ ] e-mail sign-up list
- [ ] cash box
- [ ] table and chair if you have to supply your own
- [ ] tent if needed
- [ ] mirror if you're selling clothes, accessories or jewelry
- [ ] lighting if needed
- [ ] bags for customers (as simple as recycled grocery bags or as fancy as custom screen-printed paper bags)
- [ ] scissors, tape, pins
- [ ] pens, notebook, paper
- [ ] $50+ in small bills for change

- [ ] calculator
- [ ] your laptop or other credit card processing equipment
- [ ] book of sales receipts

FOR YOU

- [ ] water and other drinks
- [ ] layers of clothing
- [ ] sunscreen if you're outside
- [ ] aspirin, bandages, first-aid supplies and your regular meds
- [ ] snacks
- [ ] charged cell phone
- [ ] comfortable shoes
- [ ] wipes and/or antibacterial gel
- [ ] map and parking information
- [ ] some cash and a debit card for snacks and emergencies

Day-of-Show Checklist

FOR YOUR BOOTH

- [ ] more crafts than you think you'll need
- [ ] kickass table display
- [ ] sturdy totes, boxes or bags to transport your goods
- [ ] price tags and signs
- [ ] sign or banner with your business name
- [ ] business cards
- [ ] freebies (stickers, pins, fliers)
- [ ] e-mail sign-up list
- [ ] cash box
- [ ] table and chair if you have to supply your own
- [ ] tent if needed
- [ ] mirror if you're selling clothes, accessories or jewelry
- [ ] lighting if needed
- [ ] bags for customers (as simple as recycled grocery bags or as fancy as custom screen-printed paper bags)
- [ ] scissors, tape, pins
- [ ] pens, notebook, paper
- [ ] $50+ in small bills for change
- [ ] calculator
- [ ] your laptop or other credit card processing equipment
- [ ] book of sales receipts

FOR YOU

- [ ] water and other drinks
- [ ] layers of clothing
- [ ] sunscreen if you're outside
- [ ] aspirin, bandages, first-aid supplies and your regular meds
- [ ] snacks
- [ ] charged cell phone
- [ ] comfortable shoes
- [ ] wipes and/or antibacterial gel
- [ ] map and parking information
- [ ] some cash and a debit card for snacks and emergencies

Caitlin Phillips on . . .
Sealing the Deal

Caitlin Phillips is the mastermind behind Rebound Designs, a purveyor of book purses. She sells her wares at craft shows around the country as well as at Washington, D.C.'s weekly Eastern Market, so she knows sales.

"When you're trying to make a sale, you want to avoid the word 'no.' When you greet people, never ask 'Can I help you with anything?' or 'Is there anything I can help you with?' Instead say, 'If you have any questions, let me know.' You want to ask your potential customers open-ended questions.

"When someone says, 'Oh, your stuff is so pretty!' it's really tempting to say, 'Thank you.' But 'thank you' actually signals the end of the transaction. You don't want to say this until they're handing you money. Instead say, 'I'm so glad you like it!' Show them why that item is special, how you made it or how to use it.

"You should practice your answers to any objections your customers might have. The right response to 'it's not in my size' is always 'I can make it in your size!' If someone says, 'That's too expensive,' try to figure out if they mean it's too expensive for them, or if they think it's not worth the money. If it's the former, suggest an item in a lower price range. If it's the latter, explain your process and how your goods are worth the money.

"When you're about to close the sale, stay friendly and upbeat. Try, 'Did you want to go ahead and get that?' or 'Did you want to do cash or charge?' And when you seal the deal, make sure to say thanks!"

THE POSTMORTEM

And that's a wrap! You've made it through the show, hopefully with a lot of sales, some new friends and a new appreciation for salespeople.

Watch other crafters to see when they start tearing down their tables—most will begin collecting their things right at closing time. Leaving a craft show early is considered very bad etiquette, especially if you just peace-out without saying anything to the organizer. The organizers will likely close the doors at the exact time the show's slated to end, but there will be a few last-minute shoppers making the rounds.

I find it really helpful to take inventory of my stock after the show to see what sold best and figure out if I broke even. Keeping track helps me be better prepared for my next show, and I can craft to meet demand. For example, I know my notebooks in the $8 to $15 range always sell out, so I try to beef up my stock of those. Make some general notes about your experience, too: Were the crowds good? Were the organizers organized? Would you want to do the show again?

Once you've sold at a few different shows, you might re-evaluate your pricing strategy, too. Miss Chief Productions' Jessica Manack, one of the organizers of Pittsburgh's Handmade Arcade, heard mixed reviews from some vendors at one show. "A few people from bigger cities said they weren't selling a lot of stuff. That's likely because they were charging New York prices, like $36 for a baby T-shirt," she says. "We wondered if we should let people know that Pittsburgh prices aren't that high."

Be sure to thank the organizers and let them know how your day went. If that means pointing out some shortcomings, do it diplomatically. Being courteous goes a long way, says Kristen Rask. "One woman was really rude at the end of the show, so we reconsidered when she applied the next year," Rask says. "It's not like you have to kiss everyone's ass, but if you're gracious, you'll be remembered."

DIY CRAFT SHOWS

No show? If you live hundreds of miles from the nearest indie craft show or simply see room for a new kind of scene, start your own! It can't be done fast, but it can be done with a little money and a lot of elbow grease.

"We didn't realize how much work it'd be when we first started, and we didn't know how big it would be," Cinnamon Cooper says about the DIY Trunk Show. She and partner Amy Carlton thought they'd just find a room somewhere in Chicago and have a small show. Then they found the cavernous Pulaski Park Auditorium and fell in love with it. "I said, 'Oh my god, we have to have the show here.' We measured out how many people would fill it—32 people. 'Can we find 32 crafters? I don't know, let's try!'" By putting up messages on crafty community websites they had the show's roster full within a month. "It was just complete luck," she says.

Faythe Levine's first show as a seller was Renegade Chicago. "It was an important turning point for me. I loved the energy, loved the interaction and sense of community," she says. After the show, she came home to Milwaukee and wanted to create something like Renegade in her hometown. At the time, she was posting daily on the Switchboards, Get Crafty and Craftster, and word of mouth helped get Art vs. Craft going. "The biggest challenge was working with a space and the logistics of traffic flow and how many people you can fit," Levine says. "It's taken me almost five years to find a space that works and the number of vendors that's good. We had a couple disaster spatial issues, with someone being put in a weird spot or misjudging the space."

Levine focuses all her advertising efforts locally. "We do local radio spots and print ads with local weeklies. I plaster all the hot spots where

> It was an important turning point for me. I loved the energy, loved the interaction and sense of community.
>
> —Faythe Levine

Cinnamon Cooper on . . .
Sponsorship

"I think it's a really fine line between DIY and selling out. When you look for sponsors, there are businesses just trying to capitalize on the movement that's already been created, trying to tie their brand with your vision. But on the other hand, there are businesses like O'Reilly Media, a publisher that's sustainable. It's up to each crafter or organizer to figure out how their brand identity and personal beliefs and business correspond with the business they're teaming up with. I have no problem with going to CRAFT Zine and trading a blog post for putting out fliers and cards. I know they're going after the same market I am in the same way I am, trying to spread knowledge and not just latch onto the image I've created."

the audience is going to be with hand-screened posters and postcards," she says. The Little Friends of Printmaking—a sweet Milwaukee-based design studio—has created the promo materials for the last few years. She's also traded with a natural food store—swapping ad space in the Art vs. Craft flier for window graphics. "It's my demographic, so it's like having a billboard up in a grocery store," she says. "I try to think of places where the people who'd go to my show go. Can that business benefit from my show? How can we all help each other? It's not just about promoting Art vs. Craft but about the longevity of local business in Milwaukee."

Across the country in Seattle, the organizers of Urban Craft Uprising gave attendees a survey to see what potential customers wanted in terms of wares and prices. Kristen Rask, the marketing director for the show, uses a blog and newsletters to keep in touch with fans and vendors throughout the year. "The awesome thing about having big shows is that there are a lot of vendors to talk about it," she says. "Word of mouth helps get some big names!" Urban Craft Uprising has craft book author signings during the show, which allows for cross-promotion with local bookstores.

ORGANIZING YOUR OWN CRAFT SHOW

If you live hundreds of miles from the nearest indie craft show or simply see room for a new kind of event in your area, start your own! The indie craft show scene has boomed in the last few years—you can see an updated worldwide craft show directory on page 200.

My friend Alisha Budkie and I decided to start our own craft show in Cincinnati to coincide with the release of *Crafty Superstar* in 2009. We had a lot of great advice from other craft show organizers to work with, but every city and event is different. Take my advice for starting a show and adapt it for your needs!

1 Pick a name. Don't pick one that's already taken, and don't play off an established show's name, like "Crafty Texarkana Bastards" or "Renegade Craft Show 2: Electric Boogaloo." As soon as you've decided a name, go ahead and buy the corresponding domain name. Something as simple as having a blog devoted to the show will give you some credibility and help people who search for your show. Set up a Facebook page and Twitter account while you're at it, and set up a show-specific e-mail address, such as yourshowname@gmail.com.

2 Find a venue. Consider your needs and what can you afford. If it's your first show, it's best not to assume you'll have one hundred vendors and thousands of shoppers. Go for something as affordable as possible, unless you happen to have a large trust fund. Ask around at coffee shops, bars, parks, churches, art galleries, fairgrounds, community centers and the like to see if anyone can offer you ample space for your event at a price you can afford.

Other things I consider when considering a venue are ample parking and proximity to public transportation. Our first Crafty Supermarket was in the back room of a bar that opened early for our show. The price was definitely right, and the venue was on the main drag of a hip neighborhood. We had twenty vendors at fifteen tables—totally manageable— but then 1,000 shoppers showed up over six hours. Holy crap; we did not expect such a huge attendance. During the show, though, the director of an arts center in the next neighborhood over approached us about having a show there. And that's been our home ever since.

3 Organize the business side. Set up a checking account or PayPal account separate from your own finances for the show, and check to see if you need any city permits or insurance. If you're organizing a small show by yourself, processing the finances as personal income probably makes sense. But if you've got multiple people involved or will be handling lots of money, it's worth exploring setting up an LLC. This will involve a small-business lawyer and a few hundred dollars in fees—check out your state's business portal for instructions specific to your area.

Figure out your costs (including space rental, table rentals, permits, supplies, payment for you!) to determine how much you need to charge per vendor space. (If you plan on soliciting sponsors, figure that into the equation as well.) The most common table size for craft shows is 8' × 2.5' (2.5m × 0.75m), and a standard outdoor tent space is 10' × 10' (3m × 3m). Make sure you allow at least 3' (1m) behind each table for the vendors to sit and stand, and keep your aisles wide enough to accommodate foot traffic (and don't forget about strollers and wheelchairs!).

Some shows charge a small, nonrefundable application fee to help defray costs. Vendor fees for indie craft shows range from $20 to $400; this is determined by the region, the show size and the show's reputation. I've seen first-time shows price themselves out of the market. Here's a tip: If it's your first show, don't charge more than $200 for a table.

4 **Determine a date.** Saturdays or Sundays are usually ideal. If you're planning to have your show outdoors, setting your date between May and September is best. Holiday shows garner a lot of traffic, so consider an indoor date in November or December. Setting the date four to six months in advance will help avoid conflicts with other shows and give you enough time to get vendors.

5 **Enlist crafters.** Post information about your show in the related forums in craft community websites and alert your local Craft Mafia and Etsy Teams. You can create your vendor list by invitation only, do a juried show or just accept everyone until every space is filled.

I don't recommend the last option—it can get crazy, and it's hard to maintain quality. Doing an invite-only show works well for small trunk shows; if you know you'll only have 10 tables, why slog through 300 applications?

Doing a juried show is hard work for the organizers, but it ensures that your show lives up to your dreams. Back in the day, craft show applications involved photocopies, mailers and money orders. Today it's much easier to keep track of applications and process payments online. When Crafty Supermarket first started out, we used Google Docs' form builder to collect applications. When we decided to charge a $10 application fee, we switched to Wufoo (www.wufoo.com), which builds simple, elegant forms and even connects to your PayPal account to collect payments. Set specific deadlines for the application and when you'll notify crafters as to their status. (It's a great idea to see how other craft shows do it and follow their lead!)

6 **Find sponsors.** Make the show a community affair. Find sponsors to help defray the financial burden, and sell ads in your program or on banner space at the show. Create a few levels of sponsorship (for example, $20 for a small ad in the program or $200 for a banner on-site) to give your potential backers options. Look locally, but also approach national businesses that serve the craft community.

7 **Find helpers.** Enlist a friend to be the DJ for the day—it helps keep the energy up! I highly recommend getting volunteers to help with the show. They can help set up tables, keep trash cans from overflowing, give crafters breaks, answer questions from visitors and manage traffic. At Crafty Supermarket, the organizers have always had tables of their own, but some shows' ringleaders choose not to. In either scenario, volunteers are an absolute godsend. Reward them with a bag of donated goodies!

8 **Advertise and promote the show.** E-mail local newspapers, blogs, websites, TV and radio stations and magazines. Send personal invites to movers and shakers in the craft world. If you can afford it, buy an ad in your local alt weekly, or try bartering—offer ad space in your show program in exchange for ad space in their paper. Same goes for a local printer.

Before the show, make signage and banners for the venue so passersby are drawn into the show on the day of. (We're also not above color-coordinated balloons.) Set up a Facebook event so you can invite all of your friends and vendors, and they can invite all of their friends. Post a vendor list on your website when you determine the show's lineup.

Enlist the crafters to help promote the show, too. "Give everyone involved easy tools to help you promote it," says Olivera Bratich, owner of Wholly Craft in Columbus, Ohio. "Like buttons for their blogs, hashtags to use on Twitter and regular updates about the content of the event."

9 **Create a program.** This could be a simple photocopied flier or a saddle-stitched multipage deal. It should include a directory of crafters with their names, websites and hometowns, information about you and the show, and ads from any sponsors you have.

When you create your table layout, "Keep maneuverability in mind when making your vendor maps," Bratich says. "Customers will need enough space to move through aisles and turns comfortably, and some of them are likely to have wheelchairs or strollers."

10 **Get set up.** At least a week before the show, let the vendors know when to arrive, where to park, where food is available, lodging suggestions and directions. If possible, arrange the tables and chairs at the venue the night before the show. On the day of, arrive before the crafters to make sure everything's in line for a great day. Arranging for breakfast and coffee for your vendors is a nice touch, too; you might be able to find a local business willing to spot you some grub in exchange for a sponsorship.

11 Open the doors! It's going to be a long day, but it'll be so worth it. Always arrive early, and wear comfortable shoes. If you have a table at the show yourself, enlist a helper for the day. Remember to take photos of the event, and having a DJ (or at least an iPod) will keep things hopping. Make some time to meet all of your vendors, and enjoy your position as a crafty ambassador.

Jamie Chan on . . .
Show Organizing

"Outsource! You cannot do this alone. Event production is a team effort, and you need lots of support. Whether your team is made up of volunteers, paid contractors or your mom, you have to make every member of the team feel valuable and invested in the event. Be a good, supportive leader, and your team will ensure the show is a success! Take care of your people, and they'll return that care to your customers."

Cinnamon Cooper on . . .
Show Organizing

"This is the most life-affirming and thankless unpaid job I've ever had. The show I help to organize doesn't earn a profit. However, every year we manage to do something to irritate a handful of people so badly that they feel the need to send us horrifying e-mails about how awful/stupid/unfair/ridiculous/unorganized we are. Thankfully that handful of people is offset by people like the brother of a vendor who gave me a hug at our first show for making his sister feel valued, or the vendor who ended up learning how to knit at a show and came back the next year knowing how to spin some of the most gorgeous yarn I've seen, or the vendors who give us high fives and make us glow from love every year. I keep thinking, "This may be the last year," and then, the day of the show when I'm surrounded by dozens of awesome crafters who are giddy and meeting each other for the first time in person, my heart comes close to breaking from joy, and I know I'll do it again."

Chapter 5

Get Noticed

You're flipping through the latest issue of *Bust*, and the fantastic crafts you see inspire a little jealousy. How did those people get in the magazine? How much would it cost to buy an ad? How come nobody knows how awesome your crafts are yet? You can start the coolest craft biz in the world, but no one will ever know about it unless you start tooting your own horn.

You won't need to hire a public relations rep to get the word out, at least not off the bat. There's plenty you can do on your own and on the cheap to promote your business. All you need is an Internet connection and a little moxie. We're gonna show you how to get noticed, get customers coming back and get good press. Go get 'em!

BE YOUR OWN PR PERSON

"Self-promotion has been the most difficult thing for me. I'm a very shy person, and painfully so when it comes to talking about my own work," jewelry maker Samantha Lopez says. "Perhaps the most valuable lesson I've learned is to have the ability to see what I do as not only my passion but also my job. Detaching myself from it in a way has made everything much easier to handle."

The first step to becoming your own PR person is to develop your elevator pitch. How would you describe your business, in just a few seconds, to someone you've never met? For example, when people ask me what I'm writing my book about, I tell them, "It's a how-to business book for part-time indie crafters." It might need some explaining, sure, to someone unfamiliar with the scene, but if a pitch spurs questions, that's great—you've got them hooked.

Online tactics

Start a blog, if you don't already have one. It's a great (and free) way to show off your work and create relationships with your customers. It's a good way to build a following, especially if you post freebies like tutorials or desktop wallpaper and pretty photos of what you're working on.

"I don't do much promotion other than blogging," says Jesse Breytenbach, a printmaker in South Africa. "I spend a lot of time reading other blogs and commenting on them. Not that I do it as promotion—I do it because it's great to be part of the community. Whenever a new person comments on my blog, I have a look at theirs and often add it to my links. I love that I've made blog friends this way—they've bought from me, and I've bought from them, too." She's also been contacted by people in publishing in South Africa who see items on her blog that they include in their magazines.

If you're going to do the blog thing, keep in mind these essentials:

- Post at least once a week—but several times a week is even better.

- Let readers get to know you.

- But don't get too personal.

- Use lots of pictures!

- Don't use the blog solely for self-promotion.

- Always spell-check.

Blog Platforms

These are the most popular and user-friendly blogging tools:

Blogger (www.blogger.com): Easy to use; free but with limited customization; up to 300 MB of storage.

MovableType (www.movabletype.com): More of a content management system; can be used to build websites as well as blogs; basic account is free.

Tumblr (www.tumblr.com): Free blogging with easy sharing. Lots of templates to choose from but somewhat limited functionality.

Typepad (www.typepad.com): Lots of options for blog experts; basic account is $4.95/month and includes 100 MB of storage.

Wordpress (www.wordpress.com): Very customizable and used for many major websites; free account includes 3 GB of storage; premium account offers more options.

Set up a Twitter account for your biz (or just incorporate a little self-promotion into your personal feed if it's public). You can also create a Facebook page for your brand and invite your customers to join. Reward your followers with special coupon codes, sneak peeks of new items and early-bird opportunities. I've got more social media advice on page 121.

Other PR opportunities

Then there are the PR opportunities that seem fantastic, but really aren't, like getting offers to participate in celebrity gift bags. Considering that it can cost hundreds—often thousands—of dollars to get your stuff into a gift tent and total exposure isn't guaranteed, it's probably not a worthwhile investment.

DIRECT E-MAIL

Direct e-mail is perhaps the best and easiest way to drum up sales. Collect the e-mail addresses of anyone who buys stuff from you and have a sign-up area on your website and a sheet at craft shows.

Make it clear that you won't sell their addresses or use them for anything other than periodic messages from you. If someone asks to be removed from your list, do it promptly and without argument. Using an e-mail newsletter service (see below) will give recipients easy subscription options. A really low-tech way to do a mailing list is to simply create a list of contacts within your e-mail account and BCC everybody when you send out a message.

Sending out a message a month to update your fans on your most recent projects is the most common timeline for creative businesses. Let readers know what you've been up to, what new projects you've been working on, the newest items in your shop and where you'll be selling this season. Make it personal—don't just blatantly market to them.

Jessica Manack, who uses NotifyList for periodic Miss Chief Productions mailings, says there is a limit to a customer's attention. "A girl I know sent out her mailing list twice a week. It was so annoying," she says. Being conscientious pays off: "When we send one out, at least one previous customer will come back and buy something."

Willo O'Brien says if you have a lot going on, you can send out e-newsletters more frequently but should space them out by at least 10 days. She uses Constant Contact and MailChimp for her own mailing lists and those of her clients. "I think it's the best marketing tool ever, but it has to be done well," she says. "If you're not providing value, people will unsubscribe fast. It's the biggest honor to have someone's e-mail address and be in their inbox."

Your odds of people paying attention to your message is higher with e-mail than Twitter or Facebook, and you're able to convey your brand's visual message better, O'Brien says. She recommends planning out your newsletters, blogging and social network messaging. If you're sending out a newsletter every month, create a schedule for what you're going to include every month, and figure out when you're going to blog and stick to it.

E-mail Newsletter Services

Campaigner: www.campaigner.com
Starting at $10/month

Constant Contact: www.constantcontact.com
Starting at $15/month

Emma: www.myemma.com
Starting at $30/month, plus $99 setup fee

MailChimp: www.mailchimp.com
Free plan, pay as you go, or paid plans starting at $10/month

NotifyList: www.notifylist.com
Free

Vertical Response: www.verticalresponse.com
Pay as you go e-mail credits or subscription plans starting at $8.50/month.

SOCIAL MEDIA ADVICE

Willo O'Brien attributes much of her success to social media. "My one big piece of advice is to give your fans and customers the opportunity to subscribe where they're comfortable. Meaning, you might prefer Facebook over Twitter, but at minimum you should have your Facebook posts feed into Twitter so those who are more active on Twitter can still receive your updates," she says. "Beyond that, it's all about building relationships. Be real and genuinely enjoy forming friendships with your customers. Talk to me like a real person, not a machine."

It's important to remember it's not all about marketing—if every tweet is just a link to your Etsy store, that's not a conversation. "Be a part of the community," O'Brien says. "Ask for advice, share resources, answer questions.

Social media's made it easier than ever to be a part of the conversation. "Be responsive to people who reach out to you via social media and don't be afraid to initiate contact with people or businesses you want to know better," Olivera Bratich advises. And be aware of what works for you. "Some people can seamlessly blend personal musings with business info in their social media presences. Others can only do so awkwardly. Find a style and balance that works for you and stick to it. Don't try to be someone you're not."

Knowing where the business ends and the personal begins can be hard. "We tend to work 24-7 in this kind of business, and our work is our life," Jamie Chan says. "Don't post things of a personal nature or snarky comments, no matter how frustrating your day was. I'm not saying you shouldn't reveal your personality to your audience, just maintain a sense of professionalism and purpose when using social media to promote your business."

"Events are sometimes easier to promote than products, so be sure to let people know where you're going to be selling your goods," Bratich says. "Build up anticipation about new products and ideas. When you're excited about something new, others will be, too." O'Brien recommends photos and polls for Facebook promotions. "When you post things that are available to the public to see, your fans can share it on their own pages," she adds.

It's also important to know when your fans are online and paying attention on Facebook. "Maybe your customers are really busy on Monday mornings, but they're chilling online Tuesday nights. You need to post on Tuesday night," O'Brien says.

Social Networks in Brief

Facebook (www.facebook.com): Your all-purpose social network—you're probably on it, and your mom probably is, too. Lots of features make it a must-have social space for your business. Create a page, not a profile or a group, for your biz.

Flickr (www.flickr.com): This photo-sharing site is fab for photographers and designers (and crafters who don't like to write that much). Tagging and groups let you share your images and discover like-minded creatives. Note: Flickr isn't supposed to be used for explicitly commercial purposes.

Google Plus (plus.google.com): The newcomer to the social networking scene, Plus seems to be mostly popular with techie types so far. But it's possible to create a business page—may as well reserve your spot now!

Pinterest (www.pinterest.com): Pinterest is a total hotspot for crafts. It's all about sharing images and creating pinboards of inspirational images. This is the place to show off your best photos, for sure.

Tumblr (www.tumblr.com): Tumblr tends to attract a younger audience, and it's all about visuals. If your business is fashion or your audience is obsessive teenagers, this is the place to be.

Twitter (www.twitter.com): Twitter users are tech-savvy and urban. It offers less flexibility—you're limited to 140 characters and an optional image—but brevity can be golden.

Willo O'Brien's Ten Commandments of Twitter

Twitter's seen amazing growth in the last few years, and every business needs an account. Creative business adviser Willo O'Brien makes a living helping crafters and artists navigate the world of online promotions. Here are her top 10 tips for using Twitter to promote your craft business (or any business!):

- **Don't autotweet.** Third-party programs can be set up to send out robotweets, but don't do this—it's spammy.

- **Don't overtweet.** You certainly want to be active (a few tweets a day), but that doesn't mean tweeting dozens of times an hour.

- **Be real.** Never underestimate the Internet's BS detector.

- **Take part in the conversation.** Social media is not a one-way street—it's important to really interact with your followers.

- **Follow selectively.** You'll seem more authoritative if you follow only Twitter accounts you really care about. Bonus points if you have more followers than people you follow.

- **Vary the stuff you're sending out.** If every tweet is a link to your Etsy shop, people will unfollow, and quick.

- **Provide value.** Share your knowledge—it's the best way to get more followers.

- **Don't start a tweet to the general public with an @.** Your followers won't see it.

- **Measure your success by engagement.** Are people following you and responding to you?

- **Use a URL shortener to save space.** Twitter's only got 140 characters to use, so sign up for a free bit.ly account.

SOCIAL MEDIA
USER NAMES & PASSWORDS

SITE:

USER NAME:

PASSWORD:

SITE:

USER NAME:

PASSWORD:

SITE:

USER NAME:

PASSWORD:

SITE:

USER NAME:

PASSWORD:

SITE:

USER NAME:

PASSWORD:

SITE:

USER NAME:

PASSWORD:

SOCIAL MEDIA
USER NAMES & PASSWORDS

SITE:

USER NAME:

PASSWORD:

SITE:

USER NAME:

PASSWORD:

SITE:

USER NAME:

PASSWORD:

SITE:

USER NAME:

PASSWORD:

SITE:

USER NAME:

PASSWORD:

SITE:

USER NAME:

PASSWORD:

GETTING PRESS

The most important thing is to target media outlets whose customer base overlaps your own. Just as *Feminist Photocopied Quarterly* probably isn't interested in bedazzled "Born to Shop" onesies, *Super Glossy Magazine* doesn't give a lot of space to hemp tampon ornaments.

After you've identified a blog or magazine you think would be a good fit, figure out who to send your press release or samples to. With big magazines, addressing parcels to the editor-in-chief usually lands them in the hands of the editorial assistants. With some googling, you can usually figure out which of the mid-level editors is in charge of the products department, and directing your submission to them will yield the best results. Many magazines also list their product submission guidelines on their websites. Some prefer mailed submissions only; others only consider e-mailed pitches. Jenny Hart of Sublime Stitching recommends sending samples over hackneyed press releases. If you do send a sample, don't expect to see it again. Magazine staffs have much better things to do than return all the unsolicited materials they receive.

Blogs' turnaround times for product features are understandably shorter than magazines'. You might be OK sending a Valentine's Day press release to a blog the week before, but *Super Glossy Magazine*'s February issue went to press months ago. As a rule of thumb, pitch time-sensitive products to magazines six months in advance. That way you'll stand a chance of hitting the editor's desk just as she's starting to brainstorm ideas for that issue. Also, consider pitching to regional magazines and newspapers that might be interested in what a local crafter is doing. They may not be as fancy, but you stand a much better chance at getting coverage.

Consider including a press section on your website where you can park press releases and high-res, print-quality photos ready for downloading. It'll make things easier for everyone.

Grace Bonney on . . . Press Releases

Grace Bonney knows good craft when she sees it. Her blog, Design*Sponge (www.designspongeonline.com) features dozens of innovative designs every day that she finds by scouring the Internet constantly and reading more press releases than anybody in her right mind should. She shares some of her preferences and advice for up-and-coming crafters.

What do you look for in a press release?

"Two words: short and direct. I read close to a thousand press releases a week. For me, a good press release is a simple, digital document that gets right to the point. Write a short intro that tells me who you are, then get straight to the good stuff: what you're making or selling, how much it costs, and why it's special. Attach a few good photos, and that's it. A great press release should rely on the strength of the product, not the personal life of the designer behind it."

What turns you off?

"Sob stories. People tell me about parents or pets that have died and that 'writing about my product would really make my day and I really need this right now.' How am I supposed to say no to that? And if I do, I feel like a real jerk. I know life and work are intertwined, but it's really best to leave personal stories out until you've established some sort of personal relationship. Press should happen because of a great product, not a guilt trip."

What do you wish more crafters knew about publicity?

"Photography is about 80 percent of the battle. Great photos say way more than a press release ever could. When I get a submission, the first thing I do is scroll down to look at pictures. If those grab me, I hardly need to read anything else. Other than that, it's good to know that short and sweet is always best. You can elaborate in the follow-up."

Dos and don'ts of dealing with magazines

Speaking from my own experience as a magazine editor, here are some guidelines to follow when contacting and working with magazines.

✓ **DO** read a copy or two of the magazine before submitting stuff to customize the pitch.

✗ **DON'T** call. Most editors prefer e-mail or snail mail.

✓ **DO** send samples to as many magazines as you think are good fits.

✗ **DON'T** CC every contact you have on a generic e-mail with a press release. It's a surefire way to get deleted.

✓ **DO** take time to formulate a thoughtful response to an editor's e-mail. Sending something right away and then three follow-ups to clarify yourself is confusing.

✗ **DON'T** take three weeks to respond to an editor's request. You might miss the boat entirely!

✓ **DO** send requested materials on time and in the format your contact requested.

✗ **DON'T** be late. If you can't avoid it, apologize in a professional manner—that means no gruesome details or excuses.

✓ **DO** condense any questions you have into one e-mail.

✗ **DON'T** send six e-mails over the course of the night as you think of more things you want to ask.

✓ **DO** ask for a contributor's copy of the issue you appear in.

✗ **DON'T** call every week asking if your piece has run yet.

✓ **DO** scan your clips and post them on your website.

FYI

Need to find *Super Glossy Magazine's* market editor's e-mail address? Go to Mastheads.org, a site with contact information for practically every magazine out there. Access starts at $4 a week.

PRESS RELEASE TEMPLATE

Press release template

Contact person (that's you)

Title, company

Phone number

E-mail address

For Immediate Release

Eye-catching, descriptive summary/headline

City, State (Date) — First paragraph states the main news.

Second paragraph gives more details.

Third paragraph includes a quote from a person involved with the project.

Fourth paragraph gives any additional details and information.

ABOUT: Describe the history of your company, your reach and what you do.

[Attach two or three awesome web-quality photos and say print-quality images are available.]

MEDIA CONTACTS:
LOCAL NEWSPAPERS & MAGAZINES

NAME:

COMPANY:

PHONE:

E-MAIL:

NOTES:

NAME:

COMPANY:

PHONE:

E-MAIL:

NOTES:

NAME:

COMPANY:

PHONE:

E-MAIL:

NOTES:

MEDIA CONTACTS:
LOCAL NEWSPAPERS & MAGAZINES

NAME:

COMPANY:

PHONE:

E-MAIL:

NOTES:

NAME:

COMPANY:

PHONE:

E-MAIL:

NOTES:

NAME:

COMPANY:

PHONE:

E-MAIL:

NOTES:

MEDIA CONTACTS: LOCAL TV & RADIO

NAME:

COMPANY:

PHONE:

E-MAIL:

NOTES:

NAME:

COMPANY:

PHONE:

E-MAIL:

NOTES:

NAME:

COMPANY:

PHONE:

E-MAIL:

NOTES:

MEDIA CONTACTS:
LOCAL TV & RADIO

NAME: NOTES:

COMPANY:

PHONE:

E-MAIL:

NAME: NOTES:

COMPANY:

PHONE:

E-MAIL:

NAME: NOTES:

COMPANY:

PHONE:

E-MAIL:

MEDIA CONTACTS: NATIONAL MAGAZINES

NAME:

COMPANY:

PHONE:

E-MAIL:

NOTES:

NAME:

COMPANY:

PHONE:

E-MAIL:

NOTES:

NAME:

COMPANY:

PHONE:

E-MAIL:

NOTES:

MEDIA CONTACTS:
NATIONAL MAGAZINES

NAME: NOTES:

COMPANY:

PHONE:

E-MAIL:

NAME: NOTES:

COMPANY:

PHONE:

E-MAIL:

NAME: NOTES:

COMPANY:

PHONE:

E-MAIL:

MEDIA CONTACTS: BLOGS

NAME:

COMPANY:

PHONE:

E-MAIL:

NOTES:

NAME:

COMPANY:

PHONE:

E-MAIL:

NOTES:

NAME:

COMPANY:

PHONE:

E-MAIL:

NOTES:

MEDIA CONTACTS: BLOGS

NAME:

COMPANY:

PHONE:

E-MAIL:

NOTES:

NAME:

COMPANY:

PHONE:

E-MAIL:

NOTES:

NAME:

COMPANY:

PHONE:

E-MAIL:

NOTES:

ADVERTISING

Buying ads in magazines can be expensive, with no guarantee of return. But at the same time, if you advertise in the right venue, such as a magazine that supports indie crafters, and use an eye-catching image, it can get your web store a lot of hits.

Before you think about slapping down the big bucks for a piece of real estate in *Super Glossy Magazine,* make sure your target audience is the magazine's target audience, too. For example, I often visit dozens of the websites advertised in magazines such as *BUST* and *Bitch* because I know they're likely to be women-operated, indie and awesome.

You can find rates for ads on a publication's website; look for keywords such as *advertising* or *media kit* to take you to the right spot. You might have to e-mail an ad rep to get the exact prices and deadlines. Some magazines offer discounted rates for indie businesses—it never hurts to ask!

If you do buy ad space, you'll have to supply the ad's image to the magazine. You'll get exact specs when you contact a rep. This is the time to ask a graphic designer friend to help you out if you're not an Adobe Illustrator genius. Browse through the magazine's ads and see what other people are doing, what you like or dislike and what grabs your attention. Generally, a clear, large image of one specific item you make is better than trying to stuff a lot of words and images into a small space.

Because advertising space isn't so cheap, a good tactic is to share the ad with some crafty friends or people from your local Craft Mafia. Sometimes you can find people on crafty message boards seeking partners to buy ad space together.

Another cheaper option is to advertise on magazines' websites. The rates are generally lower than they are for print ads. Craft-focused websites and blogs also offer ad space for indie businesses. Which of the sites you visit on a daily basis are ad-supported? Do a little digging to find their rates or at least their ad coordinator.

The real grassroots route is to trade links with other crafters. Most crafters' websites have a page for links to other like-minded shops. (If you don't have one, you should make one!) Usually, if you e-mail crafters you admire and ask to trade links, they'll be happy to oblige! Some crafters even use banner or button ads for trading. Ask your designer buddy to whip something up for you in Illustrator.

GET PUBLISHED
How to Turn Your Craft Experience into a Book

A lot of folks ask me how to get a book deal—and I love to talk about publishing. My day job is in the magazine industry, and I just happen to work with the fine folks at *Writer's Digest* (www.writersdigest.com), who've helped me out a ton.

Starting out as a blogger can help you get a book deal. You don't have to be a master wordsmith to start blogging. It helps, of course, if you like to write. (I don't really recommend it if you hate writing, unless you want your blog to focus on just photography.) It's super easy to start a blog, but it's not as easy to keep it up. Don't overpromise (like saying you'll post one new craft project every day) if you can't realistically deliver.

Blogging is a place to show your personality and give a look behind the scenes with your business. Keep it professional, though—although your customers might enjoy hearing about how you found the vintage stash of fabric for your new line of wristlets, they don't need to know the details about your most recent dentist appointment.

Update your blog regularly—once a week at least—and always include images. (Images that are your own or that you have permission to use!) The most popular craft blogs update every day, always with awesome photography.

Book publishers love bloggers because the best ones already have a lot of content and a lot of followers, and the blog is evidence they can stick with a project. Proving you can deliver on promises is of the utmost importance when getting into a relationship with a publisher.

If you've got a book idea, start with some research. Search Amazon.com for books related to yours. Make notes about everything that's been published on the subject, and explore what makes your idea different. Developing a strong one-sentence "elevator pitch" is helpful here. Rather than saying, "I want to write a book of unique knitted toys," something like, "I'd like to write a book about gothy knit toys—mini vampires, wolves and zombies—but cute!" is much more likely to get a publisher's attention.

You also have to tell the publisher why you should be the person to write it. Some companies require the author to have some kind of platform—a popular blog, podcast or some other established fan base—but craft is unique in that publishers don't expect you to be a writer. You just have to have a style all your own and be able to describe how to make the projects. If you're able to say, "I do a weekly project on my blog, Mommy's Little Monsters, and the PDFs have been downloaded X times," that's a great selling point.

I often get asked if you need an agent to get a book deal. If you aren't comfortable negotiating fees or dealing with legalese, you might want to consider it. Or if your blog is totally hot and you expect competition for the book rights, an agent can shop your idea around to editors and get the best deal for you. In exchange for their hard work and negotiating prowess, agents generally take 10 to 15 perent.

Some publishing companies won't consider a book proposal that's not sent to them through an agent. Others—including many craft book publishers—are totally fine with proposals straight from the author. They're willing to take on undiscovered writer-makers because they need people like us to keep ahead of the trends.

When you've got a killer idea, an elevator pitch, research on your competitors and valid reasons why you're the person to write the book, you're ready to put together a proposal for a publisher. Each company's requirements differ, but generally, you'll need a cover letter, an outline and some pictures. When you send your packet in, sit tight. Turnaround time can be slow, but with any luck the company will love your stuff and call you quickly!

Chapter 6

The Next Level

Once you become a pillar of indie industry, you've gotta deal with a lot of stuff—balancing your real job and crafty job, maintaining a personal life, and dealing with unexpected changes. What if you need to take a break from your biz? What if you want to go full time and become an even bigger crafty superstar? What if you just don't know how to deal with this adorably gory crochet monster you created?

You're not alone. Whatever your deal, I guarantee another crafter has gone through the same thing. That's why having a creative support group is so important: Surrounding yourself with people who can offer advice (or at least a shoulder to cry on) is vital to your crafty survival. Whether you're trying to transition to full-time crafting, considering closing up shop or just trying to stay afloat, we'll get you through it!

Once you've established your business, made some sales, made some fans, made some waves—what's next? Whatever you want! This chapter will take you to the next level by helping you understand your core customers, showing you how to hire outside help, and helping you set goals.

WORKING FOR A LIVING

Living a crafty double life can be hella tough. It seems like a good deal—you slave away from 9 to 5 (or 4 to midnight) in exchange for a steady paycheck and health insurance, and the rest of the day is yours for the crafting! But what it really comes down to is you working 24/7. How do those crafty superstars handle it?

Jessica Manack balances a very full-time job with running the Miss Chief shop and working on Pittsburgh's Handmade Arcade, which is a job unto itself. "Some Handmade Arcade staffers have jobs where they can send e-mails or work on Etsy during the day, but I can't. So I have to work on things when I get home," she says. She uses Ta-da List (www.tadalist.com) to keep track of things she thinks of during the day. "I love making lists, and I was doing that on sheets of paper, making huge lists that I'd then forget at work."

Although she stays organized, Manack feels like she could do more. "I notice people with spring lines and making a big deal about launching new products. When you're doing it part-time, it's hard to think strategically about your brand," she says. "I feel like I do a lot of just getting by. When I get home, I fill my orders and keep it going, but I just don't have the time or resources to think about expanding because my time's kind of maxed out. I get e-mails from all kinds of stores and galleries who want to carry my stuff, but I just can't do it."

Kristen Rask juggles running her store, Schmancy, and working on Urban Craft Uprising and Plush You, plus other projects. "With the economy, I'm like, 'Maybe I should get a job…' But when would that happen? I feel like if I had a job, I would get bitter and mad." One thing that helps Rask stay organized is setting production goals. "When I'm getting ready for a show, I decide what I want to make and how many of each. Then I plot it out with a calendar to see how many things I have to make per week until the show happens. It really helps!

During slow times, she stockpiles things so she never gets too stressed out. "I'm at the store five days a week at least, and I try to do all the computer stuff at work," Rask says. "I have a no-computer rule at home. That really helps, because when I'm finally at home, I can just craft, be leisurely and try to make new things and not think that I have to make something for money. That helps create new ideas."

In Cleveland, Kati Hanimägi has a more flexible schedule. "I work at my job-job three afternoons a week. Those mornings are spent taking care of e-mail, paying bills, sending invoices and ordering supplies for Oddball Press," she says. "When I have time off, I devote full workdays to my crafty life. I start my crafty day at 9 a.m., break for lunch and walk the dog, and work until 5:30 or 6 p.m." Working out of her home helps her get down to business without ever getting stuck in rush-hour traffic. "I stick to a schedule, although I do have times when I need to work late to meet a deadline or if I'm on a creative roll," she says. "My job-job is a good balance for me because it requires my time and attention while there. I don't need to take it home. But I carry my Oddball life with me all the time, worrying about this or that, thinking of text for a new card, wondering about my next marketing move."

MAINTAINING A PERSONAL LIFE

So you've figured out how to balance your day job and your crafty job. But what about your friends and your family—you know, those people you share a bathroom with. If you don't take time to chillax with the people you love, your crafty business will just get you down.

Conflicts and priorities

Jessica Manack feels lucky to live with a kindred spirit. "I think it helps to have a partner who's understanding. I live with someone who's crazy in the same way I am," she says. "He understands the benefit of my spending time on crafting."

Handmade Nation's Faythe Levine sometimes can't tell her personal life and her crafty life apart. "I work all the time," she says. "Learning how to say no to people when I don't have time for something has been a really big lesson for me. And I'm still trying to grasp it." She also tries to be conscious of the people around her. "Like noticing that craft supplies are taking over the house, or every weekend of the summer's been spent at a craft show." This way you can mediate any conflicts before they happen.

Willo O'Brien thinks being single can actually lead you to work more than you might otherwise. "It's funny how married people can use their partner as their excuse for not wanting to go out," she says. "I was having such a wonderful day with myself that I canceled on a friend, and it felt bad to disappoint her. But I feel like it would've been more acceptable if I was canceling because I wanted to stay in with a partner than if I was just staying in by myself."

O'Brien is a big proponent of the mental health day. "It's usually when you need it the most that it's the hardest to give it to yourself," she says. Making time for self-care is super important—this includes eating properly, moving your body and getting enough sleep.

For me, cooking is the first thing to go when I've got lots of things on my to-do list. I'm just now starting to accept that fact instead of beating myself up over the fact that I'm not a master chef. Buying premade meals is not admitting defeat—it's a way to make sure my body and brain have the fuel they need to function at peak performance.

When you fully throw yourself into your business, it can be all to easy to forget that you have physical needs as well. Maybe you're not a gym person, but making time to get fresh air most days does wonders for your creativity and your disposition. Make time every week for an activity you like—swimming, dogwalking, hiking, yoga, meditation, running, team sports, whatever you enjoy doing!

I think the most important thing to pay attention to when you're juggling a lot of obligations is the amount of sleep you're getting. Personally, I need eight hours a night to function and prefer nine when I can get it. Sometimes it means that I'm the party-pooper who goes home from a party at 10. But I'm totally OK with that. A friend of mine who's juggling a job, grad school and teaching yoga often gets less than five hours a night—and was utterly amazed at how she felt after getting eight hours of sleep for the first time in a long time. Never underestimate the power of a good night's sleep.

And make sure you know your limits. The big craft show is the same weekend as a friend's wedding and your dad's birthday? You could totally make it, if you drive up to see Dad for an hour, immediately go to the show and then sneak out for the nuptials ... Don't do it!

Crafty support groups

If you reach out to other crafters, you'll likely find folks that are happy to give support and advice and help out a fellow maker. Crafters are unique in that, although we're running small businesses in a small market, we don't see each other as competition. Part of this is because of the handmade aspect—none of us are making the exact same things.

Joining local groups, such as a Craft Mafia or Etsy Street Team, is a great way to keep abreast of trends and happenings. Plus, you'll have somebody to talk to when your non-crafty friends get tired of hearing you drone on about your beeswax.

Annie Chau is part of Baltimore's Charm City Craft Mafia. "Everyone who's a part of the Mafia runs a craft business. We share all kinds of information with each other—what shows are coming up, press opportunities, suppliers, business advice, anything you can think of," she says. "The Mafia puts on two craft shows a year and organizes an array of crafty events. I took a sabbatical from the Mafia this year because I simply couldn't balance all of the responsibilities of being a Mafia member with my work."

In South Africa, Jesse Breytenbach meets up with other Cape Town Etsy sellers and collaborates on projects with them. "I also co-run a craft group that meets once a month at a local bookstore," she says. "While I don't actively promote my items there, we all talk about what we do, and I've made some good contacts there—people who work for magazines as stylists, photographers, journalists. And I've met some of my blog buddies there in person, which strengthens the sense of community."

Poise.cc's Cinnamon Cooper along with Amy Carlton created Chicago's DIY Trunk Show; then the Chicago Craft Mafia took over planning the show. "Almost everybody in the Mafia was a vendor at the first show. I had heard about the Austin Craft Mafia online, and I'd felt isolated when I wasn't doing craft shows. I contacted some other people who were really into it," she says. "They thought the Austin Craft Mafia was doing exactly what they wanted to do. I was really grateful for Austin's support."

In 2008, Cooper attended Craft Con in San Francisco, thinking that she was going to stop working on the DIY Trunk Show that year. But, "I left that weekend thinking, 'Of course I'm going to do this again!' I still think about the conversations I had with people," she says. "People came up to me who I had inspired—it must be how Jenny Hart feels, having inspired people by sharing information. I've gotten so much great information from people I've never met, I feel kind of obligated to keep paying the knowledge forward to as many people as I can."

Many crafters have long-standing friendships and still have never met. Cooper and Megan Reardon of crafty blog Not Martha have never met in person but regularly give each other pep talks. "I was trying to find a certain kind of interfacing a while back, and she was looking for something similar, and we sent each other examples," she says. "Someday we'll meet up."

If you're not in a major metro area, you can find support in online forums such as the Switchboards and Craftster (and I bet you're already lurking on at least one of them). See the appendix on page 196 for a list of online craft communities.

Holly Klump landed on the Get Crafty forum via Not Martha in 2003. "If I hadn't found that site, I don't think I would have pursued building my own website," she says. "I was into bookmaking then, but it never occurred to me that I could do it on my own until I found other people who had similar things going on online." She started consigning with online shops that were recommended to her by another forum member. "Those boards were my first client base. Most of us are connected online and many crafters have personal blogs, so you feel like you know them. I think that's why it [indie craft] is more intimate than regular business. It's more about a community."

Susie Ghahremani of boygirlparty was on Craftster and Get Crafty in the early days of the online DIY scene. "Jenny Kwok from Cut + Paste (www.cutxpaste.com) was one of my first retailers—and continues to be one of my beloved retailers to this day—which was hugely encouraging and helpful as a beginning crafter with no exposure," she says. "All my fellow crafters were pretty much amazing. While many have moved on or changed paths, those crafters will always hold a very special place in my heart!"

TAKING STOCK

Your business is constantly growing and evolving. Even if you're not planning to expand, it's a good policy to re-evaluate your business on a regular basis. Nothing ever stays the same!

Part of the challenge is learning to accept constructive criticism. The business is your baby, but mother doesn't neccessarily always know best. "If you care about your business and improving it, you have to keep your ears open to what your customers are saying. After all, if they're taking the time to give you feedback about their experience, it means they care about you improving and making changes and that they're invested enough in remaining a client to see if you can change the experience they had," Sublime Stitching's Jenny Hart says. "It can be tough if that criticism is coming from an unhappy customer. Nobody really likes to hear criticism, but you'll do yourself a huge favor by setting aside your pride and listening. Then it gets easier to take, and it also gets easier to discern the constructive criticism from the unconstructive. What concerns me the most is a customer who has a disappointing experience and doesn't share it with us. Then we don't have the opportunity to address the problem and make it right."

When taking advice from advisers or experts, it can be tougher to determine whether the information is good. "If you're starting out, you can easily be confronted by people with more experience in business who don't necessarily understand how their knowledge applies to what you do. In other words, just because someone approaches you as knowing more about business, it doesn't mean they can offer you valuable advice," Hart says. "Some warning signs are that a person immediately dives into telling you what you should be doing before they've spent any serious time evaluating your business or understanding your goals."

Once, a dude started telling Hart what to do with her five-year-old company within the first five minutes of their conversation. "I listened politely and considered his advice, but I recognized it as not applicable to my business model. You should never apply advice that you don't understand or work with an adviser who doesn't speak to you in ways that make perfect sense to you."

That doesn't mean you should discount an adviser who is unfamiliar with the craft scene. "One of my most trusted advisers is someone with years of business experience but no direct relation to the DIY movement, needlework or crafting. He didn't start offering advice before he'd spent several hours listening to me talk about my business model, my customers and my goals," Hart says. "The types of questions he asked about my business were how I knew he 'got it.' He offered advice in our first meeting that I had never before considered, but it made sense to me and I could apply it immediately and see results from it. Those were all indicators that I was dealing with a valuable adviser."

> *If you care about your business, you have to keep your ears open to what your customers are saying. After all, if they're taking the time to give you feedback it means they care about you improving.*
>
> —Jenny Hart

Definitions of Success

"Doing what I love and not having to think about the bills. My quest has been to find the sweet spot of work that comes easily and relatively effortlessly, resulting in a product or service that's of value to others. I'm most successful when my passion is balanced through all areas of my life."

— Willo O'Brien

"Along with earning enough to live comfortably in Vancouver, I want work that allows me to learn new things every day and that's meaningful: Am I making a positive impact? I also strive to create positive and creative client relationships: Am I enjoying the people I'm working with?"

— Lauren Bacon

"For me at this point in my life, success is when I'm serving and building a community of socially conscious vendors and shoppers. With Bazaar Bizarre SF, our store and craft show, we strive to connect people with the things that matter in modern consumerism: shopping local, handmade and sustainable. A good show is when we see happy shoppers, local artists are making a profit from doing what they love, and attendees are learning something about the new handmade craft movement. I call that success. It's also important that the creative business ventures I pursue contribute to my cost of personal living. It doesn't have to be my sole source of income, though."

— Jamie Chan

"For me, success is a measure of personal fulfillment and sustainability. Am I getting what I need from this career? Am I doing things that I (for the most part) enjoy? Am I working in a job benefiting something larger than myself? If I can answer these questions in the affirmative, I'm pretty successful. Sustainability works itself into the mix because I want to build something that's not always teetering on the edge of disaster. Being able to look toward a brighter future also helps me in moments where I feel like I'm just treading water."

— Olivera Bratich

"Am I happier today than I was yesterday? Success! Do I like what I'm making now better than what I made a year ago? Success! Do people come back years later and buy another bag because the first one held up for a long time? Success! I'm not a millionaire, I'm working far more than forty hours per week, I have calluses, bruises and burns all the time. But I feel lucky that I get to make something I feel proud of and that people appreciate and use."

— Cinnamon Cooper

CHANGES

Along the path of being a crafty businessperson, you might take wrong turns. Has your part-time crafting become so big-time that you never see your friends? Or maybe it's not so much successful as it is stressful. When crafting takes over your life, it's time for more self-reflection: Are you happy doing what you're doing? Are you having fun with it? And, the big one: Do you want to keep doing it?

It's hard to see anything come to an end, but it's also true that nothing ever stays the same. Maybe you're moving to a new city, having a baby or going back to school. Or maybe you got carpal tunnel from crocheting so many amigurumi. Or maybe you've decided you just don't want to craft for profit anymore.

So stop. (After you've resolved all your outstanding orders and debts, of course.) If you're left with a massive amount of stuff, unload your leftover stock in a blowout sale. You can give your materials to other crafters in trades, or sell them on Etsy—it has a category especially for materials.

Liz Rosino ran Columbus, Ohio's Craftin' Outlaws show for years before deciding to leave for grad school in Washington. "I put my heart and soul and sweat and tears into that show for years. It was a difficult decision—it feels like my baby!" It took a while to hand over the reins entirely. "I started the event and covered every detail of the show completely by myself. It was getting so much bigger than I could handle on my own, and I needed to get others interested so it could continue in my absence," she says. "My hope is that it will be more of a committee-run event, and I'll definitely stay on and advise from across the country. Of course, I want to come back and sell as a vendor again, too."

For Holly Klump, life changes, market changes and a bad economy led her to realize her crafty business was creating more stress than anything else.

"When I moved to New Hampshire, I started a new full-time job and within 10 months became a first-time homeowner of a fixer-upper house," she says. She didn't want to let her business—her "baby"—go, but she felt guilty for not giving it as much attention as she had before. "I felt like I should be working on making things for my shop after work, but I could never muster the creative energy."

"The economy tanked, so when I did make things, they didn't sell as well as before, I felt like I was spending time making things for no reason," Klump says. An influx of handspinners on Etsy crowded the market, and "in my opinion, many of the shops were underselling other handspinners." She wasn't willing to undersell her work, so she did some soul searching and decided to close her business.

Klump found solace in the infinite wisdom of Kenny Rogers: "'You gotta know when to hold 'em, know when to fold 'em, know when to walk away and know when to run.' If you close your business, you are NOT a failure," she says. "It takes a lot of courage to know when to move on, and the worst thing you can do is drag it out. I wanted to end on a strong note. So I made a closing date, had a sale, and that was it." Though she was sad to see it come to an end, it was also a relief. Now that she's craft-business-free, she's enjoying knitting and spinning just for fun. "I do miss the extra income, to be honest, but when it came down to it, right now my time means much more," she says. "I am very proud of my business and I learned a lot of things along the way. With that experience under my belt, it has given me the confidence to start planning a new business. My next one will be agriculture related!"

Willo O'Brien used to have a clothing line under the name WilloToons. While she loved the apparel business, there were many parts she didn't love doing. She stepped back to think about what comes easily to her—communicating, marketing and writing—and asked herself, "Why am I not just doing that? It made me realize I don't have to do these other parts," she says. She now is a creative business consultant and the vice president of marketing for Stitch Labs. "I felt guilt and obligation to take it to the next level. But I wasn't happy doing it," she says. "Running a business is difficult, but you shouldn't be miserable."

If you decide to close your business, remember to close it down properly by filling out any paperwork required in your state. Let your faithful customers know what you are doing as you're wrapping things up, and consider leaving your website up with a message about your plans.

GOING FULL-TIME

Maybe you like the craft biz so much that you want to do it full time! This brings a whole new set of challenges, though if you're already running your business in line with IRS requirements, it'll be a lot easier.

Jessica Manack would love to go full time with Miss Chief Productions but feels daunted. "When I think about working for myself, conceptually it appeals to me. But the comfort of having an external employer who pays for good benefits is really appealing," she says. "It's a tricky choice to make when you're getting a good response to your work. You might feel like it's the right time to go full time, but in five years, your style might not be hot anymore."

If you're working with a partner, it's worth it to get legal protections for the both of you so your friendship doesn't go down the tubes if your business does.

Having a "regular" job is tough to give up—especially if you've got the guarantee of good health insurance, vacation days and a retirement plan. When you're self-employed, you've absolutely got to stay on top of your financials. You may have to report to the IRS quarterly with accompanying tax payments. (Some freelancers I know immediately set aside a third of their income in a tax fund.) When you're employed by someone else's company, it generally withholds your Social Security and Medicare taxes. When you're self-employed, they're your responsibility. Without 401(k) auto-deposits, you might be tempted to just worry about your retirement savings account later. But that's never a good idea—unless you were planning on working full-time until you're 80. And if your business has slow periods, it's really important to have a robust emergency fund.

But with being a full-time entrepreneur you also have a lot of great freedoms. You define your work hours, environment and rules. Assuming that everything's going well financially, you can take time off whenever you like to be with your family, take a spontaneous road trip or just relax. With preparation and a solid grasp on your financials, you can make it happen.

STAYING ORGANIZED

"When you have so much to do, being stressed out can be paralyzing," Willo O'Brien says. Make a point of surveying all your priorities on a regular basis and learn how to distinguish what you can let go. Willo loves using Evernote (www.evernote.com) to organize her ideas and Google Docs (docs.google.com) to collaborate with others.

Maintaining a detailed calendar can help you prepare for expected events—which will then help you stay calm when the unexpected happens. I like to think about in terms of what the future me would like. For example, when another Crafty Supermarket show is on the horizon, I have some rituals to get everything prepared the week before. I do all my dishes, change the sheets, do laundry, get groceries and ready-to-eat meals, and take care of any outstanding tasks, so that in the days surrounding the show, I don't have to worry about any of it. And future me thanks past me for being so thoughtful.

If your business is really booming, perhaps it's time to get extra help. For little tasks, perhaps you can find a student or someone on Craigslist to help you on a per-project basis or to do a weekly post office trip for you. Start-ups like taskrabbit.com were made for things like this. There's also oDesk.com, a marketplace for virtual assistants. Search by specialty and price per hour—you can find help with bookkeeping, research, search-engine optimization, customer service support, data entry, practically anything. See more about hiring help on page 154.

GETTING HELP
by Lauren Bacon

Are you spending too much of your time doing stuff you'd be happier farming out? Your time is valuable, and if you're spending a lot of it doing grunt work—or even nongrunt work that just isn't a good use of your time—you should seriously consider paying someone else to do it for you, which frees you up to do the things you excel at. If you're a designer, for example, and you're spending a lot of time dealing with customer service and bookkeeping, take a hard look at how much more profitable you could be if you had more time to focus on the creative work.

While I admire anyone who isn't afraid to roll up her sleeves and do a bit of everything that needs to be done, there's a point at which doing everything yourself is sheer madness (fueled by stubbornness, a trait most entrepreneurs require in healthy doses). Try to look a year or two down the road and ask yourself if you can keep up your current pace without falling down from exhaustion. If the answer is no, then something's got to give, and you might just have to bite the bullet and ask for help.

When it came time for Emira and me to hire our first employee for Raised Eyebrow Web Studio, we had so much work we couldn't handle it all. As naturally cautious business owners, though, we knew the upswing in demand might not last, so we waited a while to see if the phone would keep ringing. The trouble was, we waited way too long.

What we didn't realize at the time was that hiring wasn't just the solution to our too-long work hours—it also benefited our company's bottom line. Cash flow picked up as soon as we increased our work capacity because we could turn projects around more quickly. And customer satisfaction increased because our timelines became shorter and more predictable. So that first employee paid for himself several times over. I hope you'll learn from my mistakes and watch for the warning signs that it's the right time to hire:

You're working too much. If you can't remember the last time you spent your weekend relaxing and having fun—or that you worked an eight-hour day—it's probably about time you got serious about making a hire.

You're spending your precious time on the wrong stuff. None of us, no matter how multitalented, can be equally great at everything. And as a business owner, your priority has to be steering the ship, not swabbing the decks. If you're getting bogged down in work that could be delegated but isn't, ask yourself what you might accomplish if you handed it off to someone else.

You take on more work. There's nothing wrong with saying no to the wrong customers, but if you find yourself saying no regretfully because demand is simply outpacing your ability to keep up your supply, that's a clear sign you could use some production help.

You're stuck in a perfectionism loop. If your biggest resistance point to hiring help is that you fear no one else will do as good a job as you can, go read my "Control Enthusiast's Guide to Delegating" at bit.ly/HhxzFh. Then come back here and make a hiring plan.

You're already convinced you need to hire someone—you just think you can't afford it. Maybe you already know, deep down in your bones, it's the right time, but your bank balance isn't showing as healthy a surplus as you'd like. Taking responsibility for another person's livelihood is nothing to take lightly—but there are ways to mitigate your financial risk.

Who to hire

Once you've decided to hire someone, the next big question is: Who? Do you need an intern, a freelancer, a full- (or part-) time employee or a virtual assistant? What's his job description going to be? Here's how I break the options down, in brief.

Interns, co-op students and the like tend to be low-cost hires and quite keen. They're looking to grow up to be you someday, so they're appreciative of the on-the-job experience they'll gain, and you can feel free to throw them all the grunt work you want without too much guilt. On the other hand, it's hard to keep a good intern for a very long time—after a few months or a year they'll be looking to move on up. So if you find a gem, consider offering him a sweeter deal in the long run so you can hold onto him.

Freelancers are specialists who can help by taking on a specific task in your business, whether it's stitching up handbags or designing web banners. They tend to charge by the job, which makes them a good bet for anything where you need to be able to predict your costs consistently. Two caveats, though: Unless you're their only client, you'll have to wait in line, and there can be an "out of sight, out of mind" level of service with freelancers.

Virtual assistants can help manage your inbox and appointment calendar, respond to customer service requests, and perform all manner of other tasks—but they juggle multiple clients, thereby affording you the benefits of an assistant at a fraction of the cost. VAs are great for any business that requires a certain amount of admin work; however, you want to make sure they are freeing you up for billable work because they're unlikely to be producing anything you can actually sell.

Employees report directly to you, and you'll have free rein to dictate the terms of their schedules, responsibilities and success criteria (within legal limits). This option tends to provide the greatest stability and predictability, but if your revenues aren't predictable or stable, taking on an employee may feel stressful. Consider part-time staff if you're nervous about paying for (or finding work for) a full-time position—plenty of great people are looking for part-time work, and we've had great experiences hiring people on a variety of different part-time terms.

These options aren't mutually exclusive, either. Our first hires were freelancers, but they didn't offer us the stability and predictability we craved. When we hired our first employee, it was on a three-month, twenty-hour-a-week contract. (He's now with us full time.) There's no rule saying you can't try people out part time at first and move to a more long-term arrangement as you adjust to your increased capacity and new management role.

Not sure whether you'd be better off with a contractor/freelancer or an employee? Here's a general breakdown:

Contractors are great for:

- Short-term projects with fixed start and end dates, like holiday help in retail, or assistance with completing a big order.
- Filling in missing skill sets, such as drafting patterns or updating your website.
- Limiting your financial responsibility (be sure to check your local laws about contract workers).

You probably need an employee if:

- Your workload is unlikely to decrease in the near future.
- You need someone to work in your workspace. Legally, most states and provinces require you to put someone on the payroll if they're working in your office, shop or studio on a regular basis.
- You need someone who is 100 percent committed to you and consistently available.

What's the job, exactly?

Write down every type of work you do in your business. That might include sales work, answering the phone, fulfilling orders, designing new products, meeting with distributors, etc. Put each item on a sticky note.

Once you have everything written down, start grouping like items together. Ask yourself, could a single person realistically do this and that? Line up matching items in

156

columns and label them with a role. Eventually you'll get an idea of the various roles you play: e.g., salesperson, designer, business owner, customer service rep, etc.

Ask yourself the following questions:

⊛ Which of these roles is highest priority for you to perform, and which could potentially be passed off to someone else?

⊛ Where do you see the greatest opportunity for increasing your capacity and revenues?

⊛ Could more than one role be combined into a single job description, at least short term?

How to pay your new helper

When it comes to paying for your extra pair of hands, you have two basic options: Either they pay for themselves (by being salespeople, for example), or they free you up to earn more than you do currently. Either way, new staff should pay for themselves pretty darned quickly. This was a lesson we had to see to believe; we were pleasantly shocked when, mere weeks after our first hire, checks started arriving in the mail at a more frequent pace. You may have a slightly longer wait—it can take a few months to ramp up a new employee—but so long as you've done your homework to determine the most strategic hire, you should find yourself on solid financial ground.

We're certainly not suggesting you should earn untold riches off the backs of underpaid labor, but you also don't want to go broke here. So open up a spreadsheet and crunch the numbers. Look at how much you're going to need to pay them, including payroll taxes (check with your federal government for details on that), and overhead costs like furniture, equipment and so on that they'll need; then calculate how much revenue you can expect their work to generate. Make sure the numbers work in your favor.

But if you really can't afford to bring someone on, at least part time and short term, you don't have a staffing problem; you have a profitability (or at least, cash flow) problem, and you probably want to look at your pricing.

Don't freak yourself out by thinking too hard about the annual costs; remember that if you hire someone who's good at what she does, she should bring in enough revenue to cover more than the cost of her salary, and you should see that revenue boost your cash flow within a relatively short time span.

OMG, I'M ON REGRETSY?

When you're a crafty superstar, not all the attention you get will be positive. (Three words come to mind: Haters gonna hate.) It's definitely best to ignore anonymous Internet trolls and rise above the craft blog flame wars. And if some of your work pops up on Regretsy, the so-bad-it's-good blog dedicated to monstrosities and oddities found on Etsy, there's little you can do aside from enjoy the ride.

If you don't know Regretsy, take a second and explore www.regretsy.com. Helen Killer (a *nom de blog* of comedian April Winchell) posts the most ridiculous things she can find on Etsy with scathing and hilarious commentary, and her army of fans goes to town.

It's worth being familiar with Regretsy etiquette (regretiquette?) on the off chance your work ever ends up on the site so that you don't end up digging yourself into a deeper hole. Makers who make a stink about being on Regretsy just end up being made fun of more. It's better to embrace the publicity, as Columbus, Ohio, crafter Esther Hall found out—she's been on Regretsy not once but twice.

After a friend told her she was on the site, Hall was surprised and annoyed, but she was able to laugh it off. "The people who read and comment on Regretsy are usually bored with too much time," she says. "Regretsy is like a flame fest of blog comments." Her knit bubble scarf, made of an unfortunate brown yarn, was described as looking like the results of a colon cleanse.

"There was nothing to do but run with it and take advantage of the situation after that," she says, and she posted about it on her blog and on local websites. "People who didn't know me respected that I didn't take it personally and that I had a great sense of humor about the situation. I mean, what was there to get angry about? My Etsy shop got more than 500 hits after this and at least 20 new hearts (favorites) in that one day."

"At the next craft show people even came looking for me to see this legendary 'colon' scarf," she says. "Almost all of them walked away buying something of mine and didn't find the scarf so distasteful in person."

The second time she was on Regretsy, it was for a pair of deconstructionist armwarmers. "Admittedly I ran out of yarn and time for the photo shoot, so I just threw it on," she says. "Sure I had one bad item or two, but the turn around in traffic because I had other quality goods that people liked worked out just fine."

"Exploit the hell out of it and turn those lemons to lemonade like I did promoting that you were on it," Hall says. "Think about it this way: Of all the millions of things they could of chosen on Etsy, they got you, they saw something there worth spending their time to post about, even if it's in jest. You have nothing to worry about as long as you have other strong products, and of course they will always choose your worst product or photo for this site—that is their sole purpose. They aren't trying to make you as a seller look bad; they are only looking at that one picture or item. If it doesn't bother you to read the comments, go through them and see if there is a reoccurring theme that you can avoid or if it has to do with the way it is displayed, and make the changes into a more successful Etsy listing."

A lot of times, the items featured on Regretsy sell within hours. April Winchell's even been known to buy out a crafter's entire store if the concept is kitschy enough. Consider it an odd badge of honor.

Brown probably wasn't the best color
to pick for this bubble scarf.

YEP, YOU'RE ON REGRETSY!

Despite what you might think, April Winchell (aka Helen Killer) really loves crafts, and the kitschier, the better. We chatted via email about what makes an item featured on Regretsy sell and how to embrace your newfound infamy if you end up on her site.

Q: Do you have an idea of what percentage of things you put on Regretsy get bought immediately?

Helen: Almost everything sells at some point, but that immediate, frenzied buying has a lot to do with the price point. If something is under $20, it will almost certainly sell within a few minutes. More expensive things sell too, but that seems to happen more when the object goes viral or gets shared a lot. The more famous an object gets, the more the tension grows. When someone finally buys it, everyone gets excited about it.

Q: How much of those things do _you_ buy immediately?

Helen: I buy a good amount of stuff, but there has to be something really special about it. There is a difference between crap and crap I absolutely have to own. What that is exactly is hard to put into words, but I know to when I see it.

Q: What advice do you have for a crafter who finds herself featured on Regretsy?

Helen: For God's sake, have a sense of humor about it. It's not the end of the world, we're all a bunch of idiots and no one's opinion should be so important to you that you take your piece down—or worse, close your store. Why in the world would you allow anyone's completely subjective opinion to keep you from doing what you love?

The best thing you can do is embrace it. Exploit the feature, enjoy the publicity and use it to your advantage. It's like I always say, it's not important how people find you, just that they do. That's really what advertising is; reaching as many people as possible. You don't expect every single person who is exposed to you to become a customer.

And people who join in the comments and take the feature with humor are warmly received by the community. I've seen a lot of good things happen for people who approach it that way.

If you find that you simply cannot have any humor about it and you insist on being hurt and angry, process it in some way other than coming into the thread and having a tantrum. That never ends well. I would also suggest refraining from sending hate mail or baseless legal threats, as that almost always becomes content. The only thing funnier than crappy crafts are deluded crafters who think they can bully you out of your opinion.

Q: What makes the difference between someone who embraces being on Regretsy and someone who flips out?

Helen: Confidence. People who believe in their work rarely feel the need to argue with people who don't respond positively to it.

Q: Do you have an idea of the split between those two groups?

Helen: Part of it has to do with maturity and experience. The longer you sell your work, the better you get at dealing with rejection. At some point, it becomes clear to you that you are creating a product, and not having a baby.

When I first started working as a writer for sitcoms, I was really stung when a joke I wrote wasn't received well. Eventually I realized that this was a business, and we had a job to do. You cannot create a salable product week after week if you need an ego massage after every negative response. If your want to sell your work, the ego has to go. The only person you have to consistently satisfy is yourself.

Q: What advice do you have for crafters so they don't end up on Regretsy?

Helen: Why wouldn't you want to wind up on Regretsy?

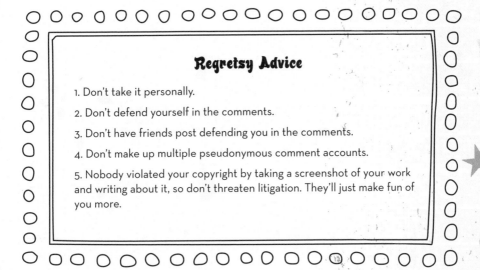

Regretsy Advice

1. Don't take it personally.

2. Don't defend yourself in the comments.

3. Don't have friends post defending you in the comments.

4. Don't make up multiple pseudonymous comment accounts.

5. Nobody violated your copyright by taking a screenshot of your work and writing about it, so don't threaten litigation. They'll just make fun of you more.

PROFILING YOUR MOST VALUABLE CUSTOMERS

So who are your most valuable customers? (Aside from April Winchell, of course.) I'm not just talking about hermione3918 who buys out all your Gryffindor scarves. I mean more generally—who are the kinds of people who buy from you?

All creative businesses—like magazines—play to certain demographics or niche audiences. (After all, who wants to be the *Readers Digest* of crafting?) Knowing who your audience is helps inform your product development and your communications. When you know exactly who you're speaking to, writing descriptions of your items and creating a Facebook fan page gets a lot easier. Does your audience have a sense of humor, or are they stoic? Are they prim and proper or supercasual?

- **Example:** You make 8-bit art jewelry inspired by vintage Nintendo games. Your audience is more likely to read *Wired*, love K-pop and be a fan of bacon.

- **Example:** You make luxe chocolates that sell for $8 each. Your audience is more likely to read *Vogue*, wear Lilly Pulitzer and hire someone to clean their house regularly.

- **Example:** You sew precious aprons from colorful vintage fabrics and hand-printed trim. Your audience is more likely to watch anything with Zooey Deschanel, shop at Anthropologie and have a bachelor's or master's degree.

Creating customer profiles—mini-bios of fictional people based on the folks who buy your goods most frequently—is really helpful and seriously fun. This marketing trick is used in lots of fields, but especially in magazine publishing (which is my day job). A lot of magazines use statistical profiles to create ideal readers, who they keep in mind as they plan coverage, write headlines or consider redesigns.

For example, my three "customers" are Allie, Diane and Jackson. Like cameo characters on *Law & Order*, these people are fictitious, and any similarity to actual people is purely coincidental.

- **Allie** is a college student with just a few bucks, but she's got a nerdy sense of humor and is likely to stockpile funny handmade cards and stickers. She's probably got artist or writer tendencies herself—$10 says she is or was an English major. She shops at Trader Joe's and reads *McSweeney's* and *The Onion*. (The bulk of my customers are Allies.)

- **Diane** is an upper-middle-class lady who likes to support local arts organizations and buys presents for her friends—sometimes a bunch of handmade books at a time. She's retired but doesn't identify with the "ladies who lunch." She shops at Whole Foods and reads a printed newspaper. (About 20 percent of my customers are Dianes.)

- **Jackson** is a middle-aged guy who seems out of place at a craft show. But he's really into craftsmanship and asks a lot of questions. He comes off as not-that-interested and then out of left field makes a big purchase. He shops at Kroger and reads mostly nonfiction books. (About 5 percent of my customers are Jacksons.)

Try writing up some customer profiles yourself! You might have one core type or a half-dozen. How do you know who your core audience is? Start thinking about the customers you meet at craft shows or the shoppers at stores you consign with. If you're selling on Etsy, check out your customers' profiles and favorites. If you have a robust e-mail list, create a survey. Got a handle on that? Use the customer profiling worksheet on the next page to write mini-bios for your most valuable customers.

FYI

Become intimately familiar with the other brands your customers love and let big corporations do the heavy demographic lifting for you!

Customer Profiling Worksheet

Gender
- [ ] Male
- [ ] Female

Age
- [ ] Under 18
- [ ] 18–30
- [ ] 31–45
- [ ] 46–60
- [ ] 60+

Location
- [ ] Rural areas
- [ ] Small towns
- [ ] Small cities
- [ ] Medium cities
- [ ] Suburbs
- [ ] Large cities

US regions
- [ ] Northeast
- [ ] Mid-Atlantic
- [ ] Southeast
- [ ] South Central
- [ ] Southwest
- [ ] Pacific
- [ ] Midwest (Plains)
- [ ] Midwest
- [ ] Outside the US

Marital status
- [ ] Single
- [ ] Partnered
- [ ] Married
- [ ] Divorced/separated

Kids
- [ ] Yes
- [ ] No

Household income
- [ ] Less than $30,000
- [ ] $30,000–$60,000
- [ ] $60,000–$100,000
- [ ] More than $100,000

Education level
- [ ] High school
- [ ] Associate's degree
- [ ] Four-year college
- [ ] Graduate degree
- [ ] Professional degree

Where are they politically?
- [ ] Republican/conservative
- [ ] Middle of road
- [ ] Democrat/liberal
- [ ] Green/socialist
- [ ] Apathetic
- [ ] Anarchist

What factors are most important to your customers?
- [ ] Price
- [ ] Discounts and sales
- [ ] Quality
- [ ] Environmental impact/green products
- [ ] Ethical production/no sweatshops
- [ ] Brand names
- [ ] Customer service

Check all descriptors that apply, and brainstorm answers for the open-answer questions. Keep in mind that different areas of your business might appeal to different segments of the population.

☐ Beautiful packaging and design
☐ Convenience
☐ Guarantee of satisfaction
☐ Customer support
☐ Other

☐ Serious
☐ Earnest
☐ _____
☐ _____
☐ _____

How often do they purchase your product or service?

☐ Once
☐ Once a year
☐ A few times a year
☐ Monthly
☐ Weekly
☐ Daily

What magazines do they read?

What TV shows and movies do they enjoy?

What descriptors apply to your customers?

☐ Stylish
☐ Sporty
☐ Intellectual
☐ Vegetarian/vegan
☐ Gay-friendly
☐ Religious
☐ Traditional
☐ Unorthodox
☐ Family-oriented
☐ Hard-working
☐ Fun-loving
☐ Busy
☐ Animal-friendly
☐ Tech-savvy
☐ Tech-fearful

What activities and sports do they do in their spare time?

What other brands do they have allegiance to?

My Most Valuable Customers

Use the demographic and psychographic information you came up with to create some mini-biographies for your MVCs.

MVC name:

Who are they and where do they live?

What's their money situation?

Why do they like your work?

What other brands do they like?

What stores do they frequently shop at?

What three movies are at the top of their Netflix queue?

What three magazines do they read most often?

MVC name:

Who are they and where do they live?

What's their money situation?

Why do they like your work?

What other brands do they like?

What stores do they frequently shop at?

What three movies are at the top of their Netflix queue?

What three magazines do they read most often?

MVC name:

Who are they and where do they live?

What's their money situation?

Why do they like your work?

What other brands do they like?

What stores do they frequently shop at?

What three movies are at the top of their Netflix queue?

What three magazines do they read most often?

MVC name:

Who are they and where do they live?

What's their money situation?

Why do they like your work?

What other brands do they like?

What stores do they frequently shop at?

What three movies are at the top of their Netflix queue?

What three magazines do they read most often?

MVC name:

Who are they and where do they live?

What's their money situation?

Why do they like your work?

What other brands do they like?

What stores do they frequently shop at?

What three movies are at the top of their Netflix queue?

What three magazines do they read most often?

MVC name:

Who are they and where do they live?

What's their money situation?

Why do they like your work?

What other brands do they like?

What stores do they frequently shop at?

What three movies are at the top of their Netflix queue?

What three magazines do they read most often?

MVC name:

Who are they and where do they live?

What's their money situation?

Why do they like your work?

What other brands do they like?

What stores do they frequently shop at?

What three movies are at the top of their Netflix queue?

What three magazines do they read most often?

SETTING GOALS

Goals are personal and ever-changing. If I wrote down my goals right now, chances are, they'd be totally outdated by the time you read them. But don't worry about timing, feasibility or self-consciousness here. I want you to write openly and honestly in the next few pages. To inspire you, here are some goals from some of my favorite creative people:

"I used to look at certain people in the craft community and try to model my goals after their accomplishments. I have come to realize that a definition of success is very personal and is defined by my personal life, which is unique to only me. I set my goals in short-term and long-term milestones. I have a picture of the kind of lifestyle I'd like to have in five years (how much I'd like to earn, how big my family will be, how much free time I have to pursue non-work activities). And in the short term, I think about the career moves that would help me to get there, and I focus on them. I have goals that are specific, measurable and traceable with a time line: adding a new show venue, increasing our gross sales by 20 percent, connecting with two new sponsors. If I'm not meeting those targets, and more important, if I'm not happy with myself at that point of evaluation, it's time to look for new strategies that will help me work toward that bigger set of goals. Be flexible, challenge yourself and don't be afraid to start over again!"

—Jamie Chan

"I have a time line of goals to accomplish in six months, one year, three years and five years. It helps me envision those long-term goals and feel like I'm always building toward something. I like to break down my goals into actions that are part of my monthly to-do lists: What am I doing this month to work toward my one-year goals? Toward my five-year goals? I keep all of these goals written out on a dry-erase board in my office. The erase part is essential because goals can and do change. If you realize you don't really want something that's on your goal list, don't be afraid to change course. For example, three years ago I was aiming to eventually open other retail locations with completely different focuses (such as books, supplies, vintage housewares). As time went on and Wholly Craft gained more customers and brand recognition, I realized I wouldn't want to start over with a new concept. If anything, I want to expand the square footage of the current store to offer more of those things and keep everything under the Wholly Craft umbrella."

—Olivera Bratich

"The problem with setting goals is that I often change my mind before I reach them. I'm a short-attention-span goal-setter. But being a business of one, I'm able to change goals regularly without having it affect my bottom line significantly. However, having a general direction and some vague goals is required; otherwise you end up looking back on a year past and regretting all the things you didn't do. And bitterness lies in that direction, my friend."

—Cinnamon
Cooper

What other creative businesses do you admire?

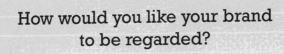

How would you like your brand
to be regarded?

Where do you want to be in 10 years?

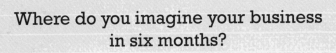

Where do you imagine your business in six months?

Where do you imagine your business in one year?

Where do you imagine your business
in five years?

Where do you imagine your business in 10 years?

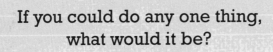

If you could do any one thing,
what would it be?

EPILOGUE

If I had to boil down this book's advice to three points, it would be these:

- Be informed.

- Be confident.

- Be yourself.

  Crafty Superstar is just a jumping-off point in your pursuit of indie business. I'm not a tax wizard or lawyer—I'm just a crafter like you—so you should definitely follow up with an expert on your financial and legal questions as you build your business. And you absolutely need to build relationships with other crafters and creatives. Whether it's starting up an event in your own community, traveling to meet other crafters or joining an online group, making crafty friends has been my favorite part of being in the craft biz.

  We're all in this for the love of craft, and our flaws and quirks are what make us—and our products—unique. No one else can do what we do, and that's why our work is valuable. Have fun with whatever you do. Make your own rules and change them whenever necessary. If you don't want to build a Martha Stewart-size empire, don't put that kind of pressure on yourself. Make audacious goals, and don't be afraid to change them as your business grows and changes.

  Talking to all the crafters in this book got me hella excited, and I hope you feel the same way. We're all in this crazy craft business together, and sharing our experiences can only make us stronger. Channel your chutzpah and be the crafty superstar you always dreamed of!

APPENDIX A:
FORMS AND TEMPLATES

Price Calculator Worksheets

Simplest formula

MATERIAL COST	
LABOR COST	
MARKUP	× 2
TOTAL (PRICE)	

For a project that took two hours to complete + $10 of materials and earning $15/hour:

$10
$30
× 2
= $80

You may be tempted to make this your price across the board, but if you sell wholesale, double this number to get your retail price. Otherwise you may find yourself losing money.

Meg Mateo Ilasco's formula

MATERIAL COST	
LABOR COST	+
TOTAL COSTS	=
MARKUP	× 1.5
WHOLESALE	=
RETAIL	× 2 =

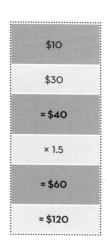

$10
$30
= $40
× 1.5
= $60
= $120

Adapted from Meg Mateo Ilasco's *Craft, Inc.*

182

Lauren Bacon's formula

MATERIAL COST		$10
LABOR COST	+	$30
ADMINISTRATIVE COST	+	$4
TOTAL COSTS	=	= $44
MARKUP	× 2	× 2
WHOLESALE	=	= $88
RETAIL	× 2 =	= $176

Administrative costs should include everything you spend money on in a year, divided by the standard number of work hours in a year: 2,080. In the administrative bucket, include things such as web hosting, legal and accounting fees, show fees, office supplies and other business expenses.

Download interactive versions of these calculators at store.marthapullen.com/crafty-superstar-ultimate-craft-business-guide.

INVOICE TEMPLATE

Your Company Name
Mailing Address
Phone Number
E-mail Address

Date
Invoice No.:

Bill to:

Ship to:

Shipping Method:

Terms:

Quantity	Item	Description	Price	Total for Item

Subtotal:
Tax:
Shipping:

Balance Due:

INVOICE TEMPLATE

Your Company Name
Mailing Address
Phone Number
E-mail Address

Date
Invoice No.:

Bill to:

Ship to:

Shipping Method:

Terms:

Quantity	Item	Description	Price	Total for Item

Subtotal:
Tax:
Shipping:

Balance Due:

SHOW SALES TRACKER

ITEM NAME	STARTING QUANTITY	PRICE	QUANTITY SOLD

You can download Excel spreadsheets of this form at
store.marthapullen.com/crafty-superstar-ultimate-craft-business-guide.

SHOW SALES TRACKER

ITEM NAME	STARTING QUANTITY	PRICE	QUANTITY SOLD

INVENTORY FORM

DESCRIPTION	COST (WHOLESALE OR RETAIL)

QUANTITY SOLD	BUYER NAME	SALE DATE

CONSIGNMENT FORM

ITEM NAME	DATE OUT

QUANTITY	STORE	CONTACT INFO	SALES

CUSTOM ORDER FORM

ORDER FORM

Date:

Customer Name:

Mailing Address:

Phone Number:

E-mail Address:

Description of Items:

Cost Estimate:

Shipping:

Total:

CUSTOM ORDER FORM

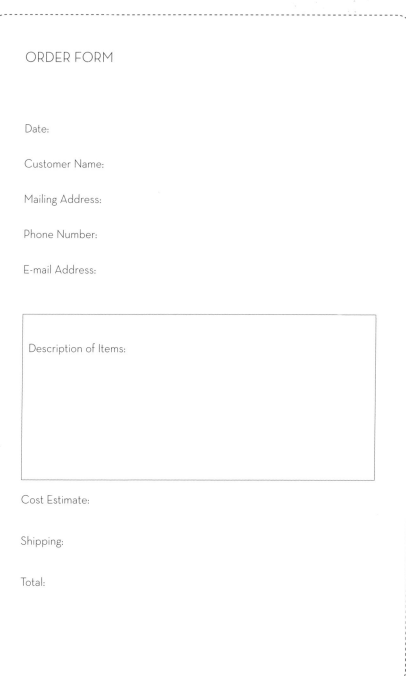

ORDER FORM

Date:

Customer Name:

Mailing Address:

Phone Number:

E-mail Address:

Description of Items:

Cost Estimate:

Shipping:

Total:

APPENDIX B: SMALL BUSINESS WEBSITES

The Artists' Health Insurance Resource Center
www.ahirc.org

Canadian Intellectual Property Office
www.cipo.gc.ca

Creative Freelancer Blog
www.creativefreelancerblog.com

Design*Sponge's Biz Ladies Events
www.designspongeonline.com/bizladies

Canada Business Networks
www.canadabusiness.ca/ibp

IRS Resources
www.irs.gov/businesses/small

IRS Virtual Workshop Videos
www.tax.gov/virtualworkshop

LawHelp
www.lawhelp.org

NOLO
(Law books, legal forms and legal software) www.nolo.com

SCORE
(Counselors to America's Small Business) www.score.org

US Copyright Office
www.copyright.gov

US Patent and Trademark Office
www.uspto.gov

US Small Business Administration
www.sba.gov

Volunteer Lawyers for the Arts

www.vlany.org

California
www.calawyersforthearts.org

Canada
www.carfacontario.ca

Colorado
www.lawyersforthearts.org

District of Columbia
www.thewala.org

Georgia
www.glarts.org

Illinois
www.law-arts.org

Louisiana
www.artscouncilofneworleans.org

Maine
www.mainevla.org

Maryland
www.mdartslaw.org

Massachusetts
www.vlama.org

Michigan
www.artservemichigan.org

Minnesota
www.springboardforthearts.org

Missouri
Kansas City: www.kcvlaa.org
St. Louis: www.vlaa.org

New Hampshire
www.nhbca.com/lawyersforarts.php

New Jersey
www.njvla.org

New York
www.vlany.org

Ohio
www.clevelandbar.org

Pennsylvania
Philadelphia: www.artsandbusinessphila.
org/pvla
Pittsburgh: www.pittsburghartscouncil.org

Rhode Island
www.artslaw.org

Tennessee
www.tnvla.org

Texas
www.talarts.org

Washington
www.thewla.org

Wisconsin
www.artswisconsin.org

Women's Business Enterprise National Council

www.wbenc.org

APPENDIX C:
CRAFT BUSINESS WEBSITES

Craftzine.com
blog.craftzine.com/archive/craft_business

Craft Gossip
www.craftgossip.com

Crafting a Green World
www.craftingagreenworld.com

Designing an MBA
www.craftmba.com

Hello Craft
www.hellocraft.com

Indie Biz Chicks
www.indiebizchicks.com

Indie Craft Show Directory
www.indiecraftshows.com

The Switchboards
www.theswitchboards.com

Unanimous Craft
www.unanimouscraft.com

APPENDIX D:
SUGGESTED READING

The Anti 9-to-5 Guide: Practical Career Advice for Women Who Think Outside the Cube by Michelle Goodman (2007, Seal Press)

The Boss of You: Everything A Woman Needs to Know to Start, Run, and Maintain Her Own Business by Lauren Bacon and Emira Mears (2008, Seal Press)

Buying In: The Secret Dialogue Between What We Buy and Who We Are by Rob Walker (2008, Random House)

The Craft Artist's Legal Guide: Protect Your Work, Save On Taxes, Maximize Profits by Richard Stim (2010, NOLO)

Creative, Inc.: The Ultimate Guide to Running a Successful Freelance Business by Meg Mateo Ilasco and Joy Deangdeelert Cho (2010, Chronicle Books)

The Creative Professional's Guide to Money by Ilise Benun (2011, HOW Books)

The E-Myth Revisited: Why Most Small Businesses Don't Work and What to Do About It by Michael E. Gerber (1995, HarperCollins)

Guerrilla Marketing series by Jay Conrad Levinson (Houghton Mifflin)

Handmade Nation: The Rise of DIY, Art, Craft, and Design by Faythe Levine and Cortney Heimerl (2008, Princeton Architectural Press)

The Right-Brain Business Plan: A Creative, Visual Map for Success by Jennifer Lee (2011, New World Library)

Small Time Operator: How to Start Your Own Business, Keep Your Books, Pay Your Taxes and Stay Out of Trouble by Bernard B. Kamoroff (2011, Taylor Trade Publishing)

Wear Clean Underwear: Business Wisdom from Mom; Timeless Advice from the Ultimate CEO by Rhonda Abrams (2000, Dell)

APPENDIX E:
E-COMMERCE WEBSITES

ArtFire
www.artfire.com

User Name: _____

Password: _____

Big Cartel
www.bigcartel.com

User Name: _____

Password: _____

DaWanda
www.dawanda.com

User Name: _____

Password: _____

DeviantArt
www.deviantart.com

User Name: _____

Password: _____

Etsy
www.etsy.com

User Name: _____

Password: _____

Goodsie
www.goodsie.com

User Name: _____

Password: _____

Meylah
www.meylah.com

User Name: _____

Password: _____

Storenvy
www.storenvy.com

User Name: _____

Password: _____

Vianza
www.vianza.com

User Name: _____

Password: _____

APPENDIX F:
CREATIVE BUSINESS CONFERENCES

AIGA conferences
and events
www.aiga.org/events

Altitude Design Summit
www.altitudesummit.com

Conference of Creative
Entrepreneurs
www.creativeconferencewest.com

DIY Business Association
www.diybusinessassociation.com

Hello Etsy
www.helloetsy.com

HOW Creative Freelancer
Conference
www.howdesignlive.com

Ignite Events
ignite.oreilly.com

Midwest Craft Caucus
www.midwestcraftcaucus.com

School House Craft
www.schoolhousecraft.com

Summit of Awesome
www.hellocraft.com/summit

APPENDIX G:
INDIE CRAFT SHOWS

United States

California

Bust Holiday Craftacular
Los Angeles
www.bust.com/craftacular

Felt Club
Los Angeles
www.feltclub.com

Maker Faire/Bazaar Bizarre
San Francisco
www.bazaarbizarre.org

Patchwork
Culver City, Long Beach and Santa Ana
www.patchworkshow.com

The Renegade Craft Fair
San Francisco and Los Angeles
www.renegadecraft.com

Colorado

Fancy Tiger's Holiday Handmade
Denver
www.fancytiger.com/holidayhandmade.html

Firefly Handmade Market
Boulder
www.fireflyhandmade.com

District of Columbia

Crafty Bastards! Arts & Crafts Fair
www.washingtoncitypaper.com/craftybastards

Florida

Atomic Holiday Bazaar
Sarasota
atomicholidaybazaar.blogspot.com

Craft Carnival
Miami
thecraftcarnival.handmademiami.com

Stitch Rock
Delray Beach
www.rockthestitch.com

Georgia

Athens Indie Craftstravaganzaa
Athens
www.athensindiecraftstravaganzaa.com

Indie Craft Experience
Atlanta
www.ice-atlanta.com

Illinois

The DIY Trunk Show
Chicago
www.diytrunkshow.com

The Renegade Craft Fair and Holiday Sale
Chicago
www.renegadecraft.com

Strange Folk Festival
O'Fallon
www.strangefolkfestival.com

Indiana

Bloomington Handmade Market
Bloomington
www.bloomingtonhandmademarket.com

INDIEana Handicraft Exchange
Indianapolis
www.indieanahandicraftexchange.com

Iowa

Market Day
Des Moines
www.marketdayiowa.com

Kentucky

The World's Second Most Awesome Art Market
Louisville
www.secondmostawesome.com

Maine

Picnic
Portland
www.picnicportland.com

Maryland

Handmade Mart
Silver Spring
www.handmade-mart.com

Pile of Craft and Holiday Heap
Baltimore
www.charmcitycraftmafia.com

Squidfire
Baltimore
www.squidfire.com

Massachusetts

Bazaar Bizarre
Boston
www.bazaarbizarre.org

SoWa Open Market
Boston
www.sowaopenmarket.com

Michigan

Detroit Urban Craft Fair
Detroit
www.detroiturbancraftfair.com

DIYpsi
Ypsilanti
www.diypsi.com

Maker Faire
Detroit
www.makerfaire.com/detroit

Minnesota

Craftstravaganza
St. Paul
www.craftstravaganza.com

No Coast Craft-o-Rama
Minneapolis
www.nocoastcraft.com

Missouri

Green with Indie
St. Louis
www.greenwithindiecraftshow.com

Rock-n-Roll Craft Show
St. Louis
www.rocknrollcraftshow.com

New York

Brooklyn Indie Market
Brooklyn
www.brooklynindiemarket.com

Bust Craftacular
New York
www.bust.com/craftacular

Mayday Underground
Rochester
maydayunderground.wordpress.com

Renegade Craft Fair
Brooklyn
www.renegadecraft.com

North Carolina

The Handmade Market
Raleigh
www.thehandmademarket.com

North Dakota

Unglued Craft Fest
Fargo
ungluedcraftfest.blogspot.com

Ohio

Bazaar Bizarre
Cleveland
www.bazaarbizarre.org

Cleveland Handmade Markets
Cleveland
www.facebook.com/
clevelandhandmademarkets

Craftin' Outlaws
Columbus
craftinoutlaws.luckykat.net

Crafty Supermarket
Cincinnati
www.craftysupermarket.com

Eco-Chic Craftacular
Columbus
www.columbuscraftacular.com

Oklahoma

Deluxe Indie Craft Bazaar
Oklahoma City
www.deluxeok.net

The Girlie Show
Oklahoma City
www.thegirlieshow.net

Indie Emporium
Tulsa
www.indieemporium.com

Oregon

Crafty Wonderland
Portland
www.craftywonderland.com

Pennsylvania

Art Star Craft Bazaar
Philadelphia
www.artstarcraftbazaar.com

Handmade Arcade
Pittsburgh
www.handmadearcade.com

I Made It Market
Pittsburgh
www.imadeitmarket.com

Indiemade Craft Market
Allentown
www.indiemadecraftmarket.com

Rhode Island

Craftland
Providence
www.craftlandshow.com

Providence Open Market
Providence
www.providenceopenmarket.com

South Carolina

Indie Craft Parade
Greenville
www.indiecraftparade.com

Tennessee

Chatty Crafty
Chattanooga
www.chattycrafty.com

Texas

Cowtown Indie Bazaar
Fort Worth
www.cowtownindiebazaar.com

Funky Finds
Fort Worth
www.funkyfinds.com/events

Maker Faire/Bazaar Bizarre
Austin
www.bazaarbizarre.org

Urban Street Bazaar
Dallas
www.urbanstreetbazaar.com

Utah

Beehive Bazaar
Provo
www.thebeehivebazaar.com

Vermont

Queen City Craft Bazaar
Burlington
www.queencitycraft.com

Virginia

Ballston Arts & Crafts Market
Arlington
ballstonarts-craftsmarket.blogspot.com

Spring Bada-bing
Richmond
www.springbadabing.com

Washington

I Heart Rummage
Seattle
www.iheartindie.com

Urban Craft Uprising
Seattle
www.urbancraftuprising.com

Wisconsin

Art vs. Craft
Milwaukee
artvscraftmke.blogspot.com

Holiday Craftacular
Madison
www.glitterworkshop.com/dish/craftacular

Canada
City of Craft
Toronto, ON
www.cityofcraft.com

Got Craft?
Vancouver, BC
www.gotcraft.ca

I Heart Crafts Bazaar
Vancouver, BC
www.iheartcraftsbazaar.blogspot.com

Royal Bison Craft Fair
Edmonton, AB
www.royalbison.ca

Germany
Handmade Supermarket
Berlin
www.handmade-supermarket.de

Hello Handmade Markt
Hamburg
www.hello-handmade.com/markt

**HOLY.SHIT.SHOPPING and SUMMER.POP.
SHOPPING**
Berlin, Cologne, Hamburg and Stuttgart
www.holyshitshopping.de

United Kingdom
Got Craft?
London
www.gotcraft.com/london

Renegade Craft Fair
London
www.renegadecraft.com/london

APPENDIX H: SUPPLIES

You know where to find a good supply of yarn, fabric and other crafty materials. But these retailers offer necessary supplies like packaging and marketing materials.

American Science & Surplus

Glass beakers, rolls of magnet tape, bulk raffia and paleo-futuristic calculators? Check.

www.sciplus.com

eBay

An obvious choice for manufactured goods, but supplies are rampant, too.

www.ebay.com

Freecycle

Unload stuff you're not using and pick up other local people's stuff for free. Can't get any cheaper than that.

www.freecycle.org

Hollanders

This Ann Arbor store has every kind of paper you'd ever want; shop online or make a pilgrimage!

www.hollanders.com

410 N. Fourth Ave., Ann Arbor, MI 48104

Hollo's Papercraft

If you're in the Cleveland area, this is a must-see shop. It's packed to the gills with remnants, oddities and every size of envelope you'll ever need. (No online sales.)

www.geocities.com/hollospapercraft

1878 Pearl Road, Brunswick, OH 44212-3252

Moo

Upload your images to make super cute and super stylish mini cards, business cards and more.

www.moo.com

Prints Made Easy

Upload your design to get postcards and business cards quickly and really cheap.

www.printsmadeeasy.com

Sticker Guy!

Making vinyl stickers at low prices for independent businesses since 1993.

www.stickerguy.com

Uline

Amazing assortment of bulk shipping materials.

www.uline.com

IMPORTANT DATA AND PASSWORDS

SITE:

USER NAME:

PASSWORD:

SITE:

USER NAME:

PASSWORD:

SITE:

USER NAME:

PASSWORD:

SITE:

USER NAME:

PASSWORD:

SITE:

USER NAME:

PASSWORD:

SITE:

USER NAME:

PASSWORD:

IMPORTANT DATA AND PASSWORDS

SITE:

USER NAME:

PASSWORD:

SITE:

USER NAME:

PASSWORD:

SITE:

USER NAME:

PASSWORD:

SITE:

USER NAME:

PASSWORD:

SITE:

USER NAME:

PASSWORD:

SITE:

USER NAME:

PASSWORD:

IMPORTANT DATA AND PASSWORDS

SITE:

USER NAME:

PASSWORD:

SITE:

USER NAME:

PASSWORD:

SITE:

USER NAME:

PASSWORD:

SITE:

USER NAME:

PASSWORD:

SITE:

USER NAME:

PASSWORD:

SITE:

USER NAME:

PASSWORD:

IMPORTANT CONTACTS

NAME:

COMPANY:

PHONE:

E-MAIL:

NOTES:

NAME:

COMPANY:

PHONE:

E-MAIL:

NOTES:

NAME:

COMPANY:

PHONE:

E-MAIL:

NOTES:

IMPORTANT CONTACTS

NAME:

NOTES:

COMPANY:

PHONE:

E-MAIL:

NAME:

NOTES:

COMPANY:

PHONE:

E-MAIL:

NAME:

NOTES:

COMPANY:

PHONE:

E-MAIL:

IMPORTANT CONTACTS

NAME:

COMPANY:

PHONE:

E-MAIL:

NOTES:

NAME:

COMPANY:

PHONE:

E-MAIL:

NOTES:

NAME:

COMPANY:

PHONE:

E-MAIL:

NOTES:

IMPORTANT CONTACTS

NAME:

COMPANY:

PHONE:

E-MAIL:

NOTES:

NAME:

COMPANY:

PHONE:

E-MAIL:

NOTES:

NAME:

COMPANY:

PHONE:

E-MAIL:

NOTES:

IMPORTANT CONTACTS

NAME:

COMPANY:

PHONE:

E-MAIL:

NOTES:

NAME:

COMPANY:

PHONE:

E-MAIL:

NOTES:

NAME:

COMPANY:

PHONE:

E-MAIL:

NOTES:

IMPORTANT CONTACTS

NAME:

COMPANY:

PHONE:

E-MAIL:

NOTES:

NAME:

COMPANY:

PHONE:

E-MAIL:

NOTES:

NAME:

COMPANY:

PHONE:

E-MAIL:

NOTES:

NOTES

NOTES

NOTES

NOTES

NOTES

NOTES

NOTES

NOTES

NOTES

THE CONTRIBUTORS

AWESOME ADVICE FROM:

Lauren Bacon

www.laurenandemira.com

Lauren is a veteran Web designer, who co-founded Raised Eyebrow Web Studio, Inc. with her business partner, co-author and all-around right-hand woman, Emira Mears. The two have been in business together for eight years, and during that time they have developed a reputation for designing elegant and highly user-friendly websites for nonprofit organizations and small businesses.

Grace Bonney

www.designspongeonline.com

Design*Sponge editor Grace Bonney has been a contributing editor at CRAFT magazine. The Brooklyn-based writer launched Design*Sponge, a website devoted to home and product design, in August 2004. Grace also runs the D*S Biz Lady Series, a national series of meetups for women running design-based businesses, which have been held in Brooklyn, Chicago, Philadelphia, Portland, Seattle, San Francisco, Los Angeles and Boston. Grace hosts and speaks at these events designed to connect local designers and provide free advice on the subjects of PR/marketing, legal concerns, business/financial decisions and wholesaling.

Olivera Bratich

www.whollycraft.net

Olivera is the woman behind the curtain at Wholly Craft! and a charter member of the Columbus Crafty Cotillion. She loves helping crafters build a living from their creative pursuits and helped organize the Midwest Craft Caucus in 2011. When she's not talking shop, she can be found laughing, performing, watching films, volunteering with local feminist organizations, and staying active in her city and neighborhood. Olivera lives in Columbus, Ohio, with her partner Seth and their two ridiculously adorable cats.

Jesse Breytenbach

www.jessebreytenbach.co.za

Jesse Breytenbach has a master's degree in printmaking and works as a freelance illustrator. In her spare time, she draws comics and recently published a graphic novel. She sells block-printed textiles in her Etsy shop, HenriKuikens. etsy.com. She tries out new ideas and documents her works in progress on her blog.

Annie Chau

www.imogene.org

Annie Chau lives and works in Baltimore (known to locals as Charm City) with her boyfriend and two darling and hilarious pit bulls. She grew up in Florida, and studied jewelry and metalsmithing at Towson University in the Baltimore suburbs. After graduating in 2005, she decided to stick around. She's also a proud member of the Charm City Craft Mafia.

Jamie Chan

urbanfaunastudio.com

Jamie Marie Chan is a college educator, small-business owner and fiber artist native to the San Francisco Bay Area. She's the founder of the indie craft show Bazaar Bizarre San Francisco. Jamie produces her own line of fiber art and craft kits, teaches art in the community, and contributes to publications such as *Craftzine* and *Indie Craft Gossip*. She co-owns Urban Fauna Studio, which is the first fiber arts studio to be certified as a SF Green Business. She is a founding member and organizer of the Conference of Creative Entrepreneurs (CCE), which provides professional development for budding entrepreneurs of all creative fields in an annual West Coast conference.

Cinnamon Cooper

www.poise.cc

Cinnamon Cooper is a proud Chicagoan, righteous craftivist, and is convinced the revolution will be crafted. As a co-creator of the DIY Trunk Show and a founding member of the Chicago Craft Mafia, she's convinced that her little bit of work has made Chicago a city more accepting of small creative businesses and more interested in handmade quality. Her political and activist interests influenced the direction of her Poise.cc business, and have inspired her more popular bags. She's fortunate to like her day job, but looks forward to the day when her craftivism pays her mortgage.

Susie Ghahremani

www.boygirlparty.com

Susie Ghahremani is an award-winning illustrator whose work combines joyful nature imagery with highly detailed handpainted patterns and a crisp, retro color palette. Incorporating her artwork onto handmade gifts and stationery in a collection titled Boygirlparty®, she's what *Flavorpill* magazine calls "The indie, start-up version of Hello Kitty." Susie's artwork is widely available in imprints such as her iconic stationery collection published by Chronicle Books and her contribution to the nature activity book series "I Love Dirt!" published by Roost Books. Born and raised in Chicago and a graduate of the Rhode Island School of Design (RISD), Susie happily spends her time making art and enjoying the company of her husband and pets in San Diego, California.

Esther Hall

tornangel012.blogspot.com

Esther Hall (Chung) is a crafter, artist and fashion designer from Columbus, Ohio. She's an active member of the Columbus Crafty Cotillion, organizer of the Craft alley at the local indie festival Independents Day and a continuing education instructor for fashion at the Columbus College of Art and Design. She has been making and crafting since she was a child when her mom taught her to crochet and sew clothes for her Barbie dolls. She's an expert seamstress and avid knitter with a love for all things fiber. She blogs about fashion, craft tutorials and daily outfits on her site.

Kati Hänimagi

www.oddballpress.com

Kati Hanimägi launched Oddball Press in July 2007, but was crafting for many years before she encountered her first letterpress. Kati studied printmaking at the Atlanta College of Art and the School of the Art Institute of Chicago before moving to Cleveland. She spends about three-quarters of her time on Oddball stuff and the other quarter as a museum employee.

Jenny Harada

www.jennyharada.com

Jenny Harada's mom taught her how to sew when she was seven years old, and she's been making stuff ever since. Most of the time she makes wacky stuffed animals, but she likes making all sorts of other things too. She lives in New Jersey with her cute husband, two cute little babies and a cute doggie.

Jenny Hart

www.sublimestitcher.com

Jenny Hart is the founder and creative director of the Austin, Texas-based embroidery design company Sublime Stitching and a founder of the Craft Mafias. She is an award-winning author of multiple titles for Chronicle Books, and an internationally published artist and illustrator. In 2012, her work in embroidery was entered into the permanent collection of the Smithsonian American Museum of Art. Jenny currently lives and works in Los Angeles, California, after relocating Sublime Stitching in 2011. She continues to embroider, make art and expand her business.

Anne Holman

www.anneholman.com

Anne Holman received her BFA from the Columbus College of Art and Design in Columbus, Ohio. She's currently a full-time studio artist as Anne Holman Jewelry Design. Her work is sold internationally at boutiques and galleries as well as online, and has also appeared in multiple books.

Julianna Holowka

www.meancards.com

Julianna Holowka was born in Detroit, Michigan, to a family of artists and crafters. Always drawing and creating, she went on to earn a degree in industrial design. Chicago was the proving ground where she defined her style—working to create stage productions, album covers, and poster art for various artists and musicians. Julianna now lives in Philadelphia with her fiancé, photographer Chris Crisman, where she designs and constructs a line of homewares and is the principal and creator of Mean Cards for Many Occasions.

Hannah Howard

www.lizziesweet.com

Hannah Howard is an artist based in New York City. She's the creative whirlwind behind Lizzie Sweet, a handmade boutique label inspired by burlesque, pin-up art and the glamour of yesteryear. An avid crafter, her work has appeared in *Stitch and Bitch Nation, The Crafter's Handbook* and *Not Another Teen Knitting Book*. She writes about the fabulous side of life and all things crafty at her blog, Superlovelyful (www.superlovelyful.com).

Garth Johnson

www.extremecraft.com

Garth Johnson was born and raised on a farm in Nebraska, attended art school at the University of Nebraska and then got his MFA in ceramics at Alfred University. He's currently a designer at Perkins+Will architects in Atlanta, as well as an adjunct faculty member at Columbus State University in Columbus, Georgia.

Holly Klump

Holly Klump has been making things her whole life and sold her animal-friendly handspun yarn from 2004–2011 under the name misshawklet. She lives in Nashua, New Hampshire with her man and animals. When not working at the library, she spends her time working on her fixer-upper house and in the gardens. Her next business will be agricultural related!

Faythe Levine

www.faythelevine.com

Faythe Levine is a maker, curator, author, collector and director. Her devotion to varied interests propels her to constantly be doing a smattering of things at once. Levine's current focus is a new documentary and book about the trade of sign painting (released 2012). She also curates Sky High Gallery and produces Art vs. Craft in Milwaukee, Wisconsin. She also publishes and exhibits her personal photographs, writing and art work internationally, in both formal and renegade outlets. Levine's first book and film *Handmade Nation: The Rise of D.I.Y. Art, Craft and Design* (Princeton Architectural Press, 2008, BuyOlympia.com, 2009) was internationally recognized.

Samantha Lopez

www.knotstudio.com

Samantha A. Lopez was born in Mexico City but spent most of her time as a child in the countryside of the state of Morelos. She moved to New York City to study at Pratt Institute of Art and Design, where she received her degree in fine art with a concentration in sculpture. Her work has been exhibited at the Rubelle and Norman Schafler Gallery and Object Image Gallery in Brooklyn. Her book, *Knitted Wire Jewelry: Techniques, Projects, Inspiration* was published by North Light Books in 2009. The Knotstudio line of jewelry can be found online at www.knotstudio.com as well as in select boutiques in the New York City area.

Jessica Manack

www.misschiefshop.com

Her college roommate introduced her to the wonders of button making, and Jessica Manack has never looked back. She's been crafting since 2001 as half of Miss Chief Productions. After trying to sell her wares at ladyfests, flea markets and zine festivals, she was thrilled when a network of indie craft shows suddenly sprung up around the country. Jessica has been on the organizing committee of Pittsburgh's Handmade Arcade since its inception. While she loves living in the Steel City, her hometown, she is always ready to hop in the car, plastic tarps and a stack of singles in tow, to check out the next fair.

Willo O'Brien

willotoons.com

As an artist, social supercollider, and self-described geek for over a decade, Willo has a passion for empowering fellow creative entrepreneurs. In 2011 she premiered WilloToons Connect, a video series dedicated to discussing creative sustainability with other successful artists. She's also co-founder and VP of marketing at Stitch Labs, a design-focused business tool for entrepreneurs who make and sell products. Willo shares her expertise advising startups, coaching creative small business owners and speaking at events around the country. Highlights include SXSW, HOW Design LIVE, Conference of Creative Entrepreneurs and Hello Craft's Summit of Awesome.

Caitlyn Phillips

www.rebound-designs.com

Caitlin Phillips has been a book lover since before she could read. As a young child, she devoured books with an intensity matched only by her passion for craft. Inspired by her mother—a quilter, crafter and Girl Scout leader—Caitlin began creating recycled art almost as soon as she could hold scissors. Caitlin's first job after high school was working at the Book Alcove in Gaithersburg, Maryland, and her love for books followed her to Tufts University, where she graduated with a double major in English and drama. In 2004, Rebound Designs was born, and Caitlin began selling her crafty creations full time at the historic Eastern Market in Washington, D.C. Caitlin also exhibits at a variety of shows, from the funky Crafty Bastards in D.C. to the prestigious American Craft Council Show in Baltimore.

Kristen Rask

www.schmancytoys.com

Kristen Rask was born in Cleveland, Ohio. In 1998, she landed in Seattle, which she has made her home. In 2004, she opened a small store in downtown Seattle called Schmancy, where she sells vinyl and plush toys and other crafty goods. Since her opening, she has been invited to curate art shows from New York City to San Francisco. She curates an annual show, Plush You!, at her store (and a few others), which received so much attention that North Light Books published the book *Plush You!* in 2007. She is also the author of *Button and Stitch* (North Light Books, 2009). She is the president of Seattle's largest indie craft show, Urban Craft Uprising. Her fourth book, *Yummy Crochet,* came out in fall of 2010 and is already in reprint.

INDEX

DEDICATION

For my crafty grandmas, Frances and Marian.

ABOUT THE AUTHOR

Grace Dobush is a writer, editor and crafter based in Cincinnati, Ohio. By day, she's the executive editor of HOWInteractiveDesign.com and the community manager for *HOW* and *Print* magazines. By night, she's a co-organizer of Cincinnati's biannual Crafty Supermarket, and she's sold her handbound books and linocut cards at shows around the country. A proud alumna of Kent State's journalism school, Grace has written about craft, art, design and other random things for *Wired*, *HOW*, *Family Tree Magazine* and *The Artist's Magazine*, among others. Learn more at www.craftysuperstar.com, and keep up to date with her on Facebook at www.facebook.com/craftysuperstar and on Twitter at @GraceDobushToGo!

www.fwmedia.com

16   15   14   13   12   5   4   3   2   1

DISTRIBUTED IN CANADA BY FRASER DIRECT
100 Armstrong Avenue
Georgetown, ON, Canada L7G 5S4
Tel: (905) 877-4411

DISTRIBUTED IN THE U.K. AND EUROPE BY F&W MEDIA
INTERNATIONAL
Brunel House, Newton Abbot, Devon, TQ12 4PU, England
Tel: (+44) 1626 323200, Fax: (+44) 1626 323319
E-mail: enquiries@fwmedia.com

DISTRIBUTED IN AUSTRALIA BY CAPRICORN LINK
P.O. Box 704, S. Windsor NSW, 2756 Australia
Tel: (02) 4577-3555

ISBN 13: 978-1-4403-2037-8
SRN: W7388

Editor: Rachel Scheller
Designer: Charly Bailey
Production Coordinator: Greg Nock
Illustrator: Ron Warnick

GET ORGANIZED!

Download these über-useful forms to whip your craft business into shape:

⊙ Craft Biz Budget Tracker: Make the math easy. Track your income and expenses with this interactive spreadsheet.

⊙ Craft Show Application Tracker: Who needs a filing cabinet? Keep all your pending and accepted application info in one spot.

⊙ Customer Profiling Worksheet: Just who are you selling to? Learn about your customer with this user-friendly worksheet.

⊙ Pricing Formulas: Calculate prices for your handmade items with three different formulas in this interactive spreadsheet.

⊙ Sales Tax Cheat Sheet: Taxes got you stumped? Calculate and record sales tax rates for different cities so you always know how much to charge, no matter where you're selling.

To access all the forms, go to http://store.marthapullen.com/crafty-superstar-ultimate-craft-business-guide

Get your craft on at store.marthapullen.com. Find inspiring craft books, materials, notions and more!

Join the online crafting community!

 facebook.com/fwcraft

 @fwcraft